RE-WILD

To Mariasole.
                S.L.T.

Publisher
Balthazar Pagani

Editing
Caterina Grimaldi

Graphic Design
Davide Canesi / PEPE *nymi*

Editorial assistant
PEPE *nymi*

Vivida

Vivida™ is a trademark property of White Star s.r.l.
www.vividabooks.com

© 2022 White Star s.r.l.
Piazzale Luigi Cadorna, 6
20123 Milan, Italy
www.whitestar.it

Translation: ICEIGeo, Milan (translation: Cynthia Anne Koeppe)
Editing: Phillip Gaskill

1 2 3 4 5 6   26 25 24 23 22

Copyright 2022 by Virginia Taroni.
Published by Mango Publishing, a division of Mango Publishing Group, Inc.
Library of Congress Cataloging-in-Publication number: 2022937334
ISBN: (print) 978-1-68481-037-6 \ (ebook) 978-1-68481-038-3

Stefano Luca Tosoni

RE-WILD

50 PATHS TO RECONNECT WITH NATURE

Illustrations by
Virginia Taroni

mango
PUBLISHING GROUP

CONTENTS

③ **FEEDING YOURSELF WITH NATURE**

④ **IN THE WILD**

⑤ EXPERIENCING NATURE

Preface

by **Valeria Margherita Mosca**

....

Stefano is very special to me. He is my most trusted travel companion, with whom I share a great number of projects and most of the values that make our lives similar.

Since we spend a lot of time together, we often talk about what we are experiencing, what we are thinking, what we are dreaming about, and what we are creating by making our wishes come true. I can confirm with certainty (and a touch of pride) that I watched as this book was born, and I watched it grow until today, the day of its publication.

Over recent months, the words he has used to describe his research and the experiences that brought him to write this book have become great, positive stimuli for reflection and change in me. With those words, Stefano has become the spokesperson for the empathy between man and nature, a valuable resource that is disappearing in a historic moment, a resource that has come to be thought of in a way that is too fashionable and superficial.

I am a forager, a guide, and an environmental researcher. I do not directly investigate the themes that make up this book, but I have been closely observing the world of nature with love and passion for many years now. I study it, I catalogue it, and I explore it. Of course my perspective is different from Stefano's, but often our views inexorably meet in the anthropological and ecological intrigue that defines man's relationship with the biosphere. After all is said and done, we both simply feel great admiration, love, and respect for natural dynamics and for all of the planet's forms of life.

The story of these values, which are well rooted in his heart, begins a long time ago. When Stefano was just a child, he embarked on marvelous trips and true adventures with his parents; many of these were in the middle of an intense, uncontaminated nature that is still alive and present, both in his real experiences and in the world of his boundless imagination. With her sweetness and strength, his mother taught him the perseverance and resilience he needed to reach any goal, while his father taught him how to live life with enthusiasm and positivity. He taught him how to accept challenges, to explore, to look at all the infinite possibilities with curiosity, and to see the world as a place to love deeply. It was with his father, in particular, that he lived the adventures that inspired this book and that taught him to be on the side of nature.

Like Stefano, I also shared this inclination as a child, with my maternal grandmother and my parents. I have two special memories that take me back to the origins of my passion and to this almost shamanic generational exchange (like an inner pact) between a little girl and nature.

The first takes me back to the first time I had the idea of putting some leaves and fir branches in a frying pan. I was huddled over the grass under a terrace of my house in Valmalenco, a beautiful uncontaminated side valley of the Valtellina, in northern Italy. I had just come back from a long wander in the nearby forest, where I had admired the towering trunks of the fir trees and larches that rose up into the sky. I was hopelessly fascinated and could not help but ask myself if a plant that evoked the flavor of adventures and freedom could possibly have the same intoxicating, inebriating taste as the smell that my nose perceived in the air, a smell that so inexorably attracted my chemical receptors. So I began to fantasize and cook for play, filling my little pots with needles, bark, lichens, and leaves, and to make notes about my explorations in a notebook where I drew maps and described the plants and minerals I found.

My second memory is one of what happened a few days after my first cooking experiments. As I observed my grandmother, whose ancestors came from a completely unspoiled valley, the Val Zebrù, I realized that she looked for and picked the same plants I had cooked for play in my unusual recipes, and she used what she gathered to prepare tisanes, remedies, and delicious banquets with what she harvested, with the profound knowledge of the elderly. From that day on, picking wild plants became part of my daily life. Viewing the forest as an edible landscape to explore and with which to practice a respectful exchange became a habit and, a few years later, my job. To gather the edible ingredients that the forest offers, you must be able to identify the plant species that grow there, and get to know its complex, fascinating, delicate ecosystem, and learn to respect it.

I believe that Stefano's experience and mine, with our respective parents and grandparents, were very similar. In sharing their life experiences and their wealth of knowledge with us, our ancestors gave us the love and the sense of belonging and care that only the experiences of life lived together can bring. But above all, they taught us how to have a respectful, fruitful exchange with the biosphere, an exchange that translates to the very important, but often abused, terms of environmental knowledge, protection, and cooperation. They taught us to observe nature in its smallest details, from an intimate, trusting perspective, real enough to instill in us the strength and will to become messengers and advocates, defenders of the planet, and spokespeople for its beauty and its needs.

Stefano's book is a vehicle for this great mission. It provides us with delicate, enjoyable ways to reconnect that are refined but adventurous. For the most attentive and sensitive reader, the book will be a one-way trip to a more complete and conscious future.

Introduction

....

The idea for this book formed many years ago, in the English Midlands, during a business trip to a company that designs and develops video games. The schedule included a morning of meetings in a room overlooking the splendid English countryside, which could be seen in all its beauty outside a large window.

During the meeting, the other guests and I watched spectacular changes of the color of the sky, the quick passing of clouds, and short bursts of rain interspersed with the sudden clearings that are typical of certain days in England. The more amazed I was, the more details I was able to observe: species of birds that were unknown to me; winds that lashed the grass, creating concerted, harmonious movements and shades of color and ever-changing hues that stretched all the way to the horizon.

The show that nature was putting on that day was a sharp contrast to the plots of the video games that were being demonstrated for us: scenarios of cyberpunk, fantasy, and science fiction made even more complex by the technical details we were receiving from the programmers. In a nearby field, a boy and girl suddenly appeared. They were walking leisurely in the high grass under a steady rain, protected by rubber boots, raincoats, and waterproof hats. I looked at their faces for signs of distress caused by the rain and wind and was surprised to see that they were completely comfortable as they engaged in what looked to be a funny conversation, totally undisturbed by the weather.

The scene attracted the attention of those of us in the meeting, and a manager explained that the couple were part of the digital creative team, who create characters and imaginary environments. Just as the other employees did, they had permission to leave their desks whenever they felt the need to go outside to take a walk, or to lie down in the grass on a sunny day, to freely enjoy the air and the rain.

When we were touring the company in the afternoon, we noticed a row of colorful raincoats and rubber boots lined up in the entry hall, as well as wet tracks that led in the direction of the locker rooms where there are showers and saunas. The employees not only had permission to adventure into the countryside; they were encouraged to do so.

Later, a modeler told me that his job was to reconstruct the plants and animals in the scenarios of a famous rally game. The goal was to accurately recreate the biodiversity in the various scenarios. This required a thorough understanding of plants and of the way each area behaves with a change in seasons or atmospheric conditions. After enthusiastically showing me his primary source, an old volume where the world's trees and wild botanical species of the Northern Hemisphere were catalogued, he confirmed that the company invited employees to explore their natural surroundings in the belief that this would positively affect their job performance. Nature was seen as more than something to be studied: it was a resource to improve focus, the team spirit, health, and, more generally speaking, the health of each employee.

I went home with a new awareness that I felt I needed to explore further. Since then, I have experienced moments that are among my most precious memories. This new bond with nature that I sought out has brought back many experiences of my childhood; it has helped me evolve, just as my knowledge of nature itself has evolved and has led me to believe that happiness and the meaning of life come directly from it.

After many years, these were the reasons that drove me to write this book. It includes a collection of activities that are within everyone's reach, activities that are designed to be done outdoors, not just surrounded by nature, but actively seeking contact and interacting with it.

This book will accompany you step by step as you observe, take notes, and participate in activities that will allow you to rediscover the innate bond each of us has with our natural environment—the trees, the plants, the forests, and the animals. The bond is always there, ready to be nurtured and strengthened.

The time has come to let our wild side develop, the side that allows us to feel at home even outside of our homes. The re-wilding path has given me a great deal, and I hope it can do the same for those of you who will read this book.

Chapter 1

GETTING TO KNOW NATURE

A Forest in Your Head

....

The *Nature of Americans* study, coordinated by Prof. Stephen R. Kellert of the Yale School of Forestry & Environmental studies, showed that adults and children spend an average of five hours a week outdoors, approximately one-tenth of the time spent outdoors sixty years ago. At the same time, the amount of time spent using electronic screen devices such as cell phones, PCs, or televisions is more than four and a half hours a day. The data are similar for all the world's industrialized countries, and they point to a rapid decline in our contact with nature.

If we consider the historic and social phases of the last century that led us to where we are today, we can deduce that this phenomenon primarily involves the two latest generations. The relationship our grandparents had with nature was closer and deeper. Their cities were more sparsely populated, and they often lived in small burgs or farms in the middle of fields and forests. At least until the middle of the last century, nature was a fundamental element for those who lived in these contexts: it provided food, cures, entertainment, and work.

Today, on the other hand, going outside to take a walk in the woods or going to the park is considered a moment of recreation that is in direct competition with the time that should be dedicated to studies, work, and our daily tasks. During the day, the free time each of us has is fragmented into a series of short pauses that we use to write personal e-mails, post on social media, read a book, play a video game, or watch television. We rarely take advantage of these pauses to get outside and plunge into the nature that surrounds us.

To make matters worse, since the beginning of the century, the environments where we live, study, work, and play have become almost completely artificial. Sidewalks, roads, buildings, and trees are placed as objects in the urban design that make up an environment we have come to consider normal, an environment that is more familiar to us than a pine forest or a mountain brook.

We think of guided meditation with the sounds of the forest that we can watch on YouTube, or of screensavers of spectacular waterfalls, or woods lit up with the first rays of sun. We resort to these tools because we often prefer to observe and *experience* natural environments through the contents available on our electronic devices, rather than actually diving into them in real life. Similarly, our children follow science programs at school that prefer to describe nature with theory lessons, rather than go outside in the open air and experience nature firsthand. This approach leads to the complete loss of contact with reality and with the true essence of our planet—its physicality, its rawness, and its fierce but wondrous authenticity.

These habits have made us insensitive to all the things that we perceive as being outside of ourselves; and nature is one of those things. Consequently, we pay little attention to the environmental crises that are taking place just a few hours' drive from our homes—such as the melting of glaciers or the progressive desertification of areas that until a few years ago were prosperous and rich.

The result is that we become helpless bystanders to the rapid upheaval of natural balances, failing to realize the urgency with which we must change our lifestyles, almost as if this upheaval will have no effect on our survival.

However, with the recent global health emergency, things seem to be changing. The restrictions imposed on our freedom to move about due to the spread of the COVID-19 virus have led us to rediscover the value of living more naturally and the need to establish a deeper relationship with the reality that surrounds us.

The goal of this book is to provide instruments that help us rediscover the role nature plays in our lives. We need to dedicate time to nature, because staying in a relationship with our environment is a fundamental necessity to living our lives as best we can. Keeping in contact with nature and spending time outdoors is relaxing, it increases our propensity to socialize, it strengthens our immune system, and it nurtures our sensitivity to issues concerning environmental protection and the preservation of ecosystems. Re-establishing contact with the environment does not necessarily mean going back to living like our ancestors. We need to find a new, modern way that allows us to play an active role in the mechanisms that regulate our habitat but, at the same time, keep in step with our social and cultural evolution.

There is still time for us to rediscover the most instinctual, creative, empathetic, and collaborative sides of our nature as human beings. We can begin by reclaiming our time and skills, restoring the basics that allow us to rediscover the environment and the importance of being in touch with it, which will in turn allow us to develop a sense of responsibility toward nature. Let's start to reconnect! Happy travels!

Let's start to reconnect! Happy travels!

Get ready for a trip that will take us outdoors to discover our true natural essence.

Your Travel Journal

For decades before the advent of digital photography, explorers filled their suitcases with notebooks, pencils, watercolors, and whatever else they needed to document the things that captured their attention. The traveler was often a true explorer—an anthropologist, an archeologist, or a botanist who generally traveled for firsthand research. So, at a time when it was impossible to photograph landscapes, animals, archeological ruins, plants, fruit, flowers, or insects they discovered during their explorations, their only alternative was to draw, sketch, take notes, and glue their findings in notebooks in order to have sufficient materials to take home with them.

When he was just twenty-two years old, the famous naturalist Charles Darwin was contacted by the esteemed botanist and entomologist John Stevens Henslow. On August 25, 1831, Henslow wrote him a letter in which he proposed an expedition aboard the ship *HMS Beagle*. He wrote, "I have stated that I consider you to be the best qualified person I know of who is likely to undertake such a situation—I state this not on the supposition of your being a finished Naturalist, but as amply qualified for collecting, observing, & noting anything worthy to be noted in Natural History."

During the trip aboard the *Beagle*, Darwin catalogued hundreds of species in his journal, observing characteristics and specificities, and compiling the information he would use in the following years to elaborate and better define his theory of evolution. Along our pathway to re-establishing our connection with nature, we will see and discover a myriad of interesting elements to document with notes and drawings, or with findings of what we encounter, glued into our journal. The journal does not need to be anything elaborate. I suggest choosing one with pages of a good weight that will withstand the use of light watercolors or dark ink.

Start taking notes in your journal under today's date, the beginning of your journey.

Breathing

The first and last action you will carry out as a living creature is to breathe. Breathing is what most defines us as living creatures: plants, people, and animals are all characterized by this spontaneous, cyclical, perfect act.

The so-called Gaia hypothesis was formulated by the British chemist James Lovelock and the American biologist Lynn Margulis in 1979. According to the theory, living organisms interact with their inorganic surroundings on Earth to form a synergistic and self-regulating complex system that helps to maintain and perpetuate the conditions for life on the planet. Nature takes the form we know, and works this way, exclusively because it is organized to react to the presence of oxygen, and breathing is both the primary response and the driving force of this type of organization.

Everything around us moves in a continuous flow of inhalations and exhalations, and the circularity of this *in-out* movement is a useful key to reflect on the fact that everything on our planet follows the same circular dynamic. Paying attention to our breathing is a simple way to learn that an action corresponds to an opposite reaction; for every birth, there is an adieu; for every dawn, there is a sunset; and so on. Everything ends and begins again; everything dies and is recreated, which suggests that existence itself follows a principle of cyclicity and repetition.

Breathing makes us aware of being alive and allows us to understand the value of our experience on earth. We are part of a large complex system that works when people, animals, insects, and plants all breathe together.

Find a suitable place in your house or outdoors where you can focus on your breathing. Close your eyes and feel the air as it passes through your nose to your lungs, stays suspended for a moment, and then goes back out of your body, warmer. Try to feel your body as it moves, and imagine that you are breathing together with all the other living creatures on the planet. Try to imagine the earth itself breathing, in one concerted inhale and exhale; then open your eyes and let the gratitude in.

The World Wakes Up

It is the moment when nature wakes up, birds start singing, and plants change their breathing and begin to produce oxygen. The silence of the night that carries over into the morning allows us to appreciate the world from a different point of view that is more absolute and solemn. Sunrise and sunset are two very symbolic moments for nature and for life. The sunrise evokes rebirth, renewal, and new departures, while sunset evokes arrival, the suspension of time, and the end of a cycle.

It is no secret that these splendid moments in the day, when time stands still, give us a moment of special refuge conducive to self-reflection—an inner awakening that helps us connect to nature and understand the mechanisms that regulate the way it works. What we know today as *sungazing*, the act of looking directly into the sun during the hours in which its light is least intense, is an ancient practice known to the Egyptians, Mayans, Aztecs, Tibetans, and some Native American cultures as a method of caring for the mind and enriching the spirit.

Using the shadows of trees and houses to observe when and where the sun comes up on the horizon is a simple way to understand that the planet we live on undergoes cyclical changes, and to get in tune with the rhythms of nature.

Set your alarm for ten minutes before sunrise, look for a window or observation point to the east, observe, and take note.

SUNRISE

The sun rises in the east and sets in the west, but only during the spring and autumn equinoxes. During the winter solstice, the sun rises in the southeast and sets in the southwest; and during the summer solstice, the sun rises in the northeast and sets in the northwest.

What we consider simply as the sunrise is actually an event made of other small, shorter moments. From the night, we pass into the *astronomic twilight*, which corresponds to the moment in which the sky is no longer totally dark and the sun begins to rise, still 18 degrees below the horizon. A small part of the sun's rays already illuminate the highest layers of the atmosphere, the less luminous stars begin to disappear, and the earliest birds, such as the redstart and the thrush, begin to sing.

The next phase is the *nautical twilight*, in which the sun rises to about 12 degrees below the horizon. It is known as such because the sky becomes lighter than the sea and the land, which makes it possible to navigate by sight. This is the time when other birds, such as the blackbird, robin, and wren, wake up and join in the concert of chirps.

The final phase is *civil twilight*, when there is enough natural light to begin human activities without resorting to artificial illumination. In this phase, when the sun is about 6 degrees below the horizon, the *aurora* appears as golden and sometimes pink, purple, or copper-colored light in the sky just before sunrise.

These colors are the result of light refracted through the lower layers of the atmosphere. The final phase ends when the sun rises up from the horizon and a new day begins.

Let's Go Outside!

The time has come for us to approach our first exploration, so we need to prepare properly, choosing clothes that are suitable for the temperature and weather conditions predicted for the day. To dive into an unspoiled environment outside the city, we need to choose an itinerary, consult a map to see what paths we can take, check for shelters or bivouacs we can go to if necessary, and make someone aware of our plans before leaving, especially if we are going on our excursion alone. In some places, no cell phone service will be available to make or receive calls, so we must think first and foremost about safety. Check more than one source for the weather forecast to avoid surprises. There are a number of very accurate websites.

Depending on the season, it is advisable to opt for clothing that will withstand humidity, heat, cold, or rain. Choosing the right clothing and equipment depends above all on the type of destination you are visiting and the predicted weather conditions.

For example, if our destination is in the high mountains, temperatures will be low even in the summer, and we will need to use climbing spurs and walking poles for glacier hiking. If we are considering climbing as well, we will need special equipment and the help of an excursion buddy.

We should think of our clothing as a series of "onion peel" layers that we can take off and put on as necessary. Taking a waterproof jacket is always a good idea. We must never forget to put food and water in our backpacks; something caloric will give us energy when we are unable to reach a shelter or a refreshment area. And last but not least, we need to choose suitable shoes that are resistant, with rubber soles that give you a good grip on the ground and keep your feet warm and dry for the duration of the hike.

Let's go exploring! Don't forget your journal; pencil or pen for writing and drawing; some tape or glue to stick your finds to the pages; and a camera to document what catches your eye—each an essential part of your equipment.

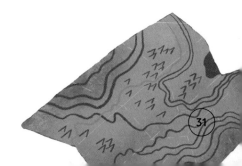

Observing What We Have Around Us

Paying attention to the nature that surrounds us deeply influences our state of mind, our level of happiness and connection, and the empathy we have for others. This is the result, in brief, of a study conducted by Holli-Anne Passmore, PhD, in the department of Psychology at the University of British Columbia in Okanagan, Canada. The study demonstrates how the observation of nature can influence people's well-being, whether they live in a city or in a less contaminated environment.

The study was published in 2016 in the *Journal of Positive Psychology*. It involved 395 volunteers, divided into two groups. The first group was asked to take a series of photos of plants, herbs, animals, trees, and any other natural element that they found during their daily routine, and, as they did so, to note in a journal how their state of mind responded to this careful observation. The second group was asked to focus their attention on artificial elements such as buildings, statues, sidewalks, streetlamps, and so forth. The result was that the level of happiness and well-being of the participants and their sense of connection to others was significantly higher for the group that had focused on natural elements.

As the day goes by, look for trees that grow around us, wild plants and animals, and observe how the clouds move, the direction of the wind, and how dusk advances a bit at a time. Observe houseplants, rays of sunlight as they hit surfaces, the changes in the color of the grass as the seasons change, and any other natural element that helps you understand the true vitality of our world and the sense of joy and fulfillment it can bring if we focus on the right things.

In your journal, you can note the characteristics of the natural elements that catch your eye during the day: a tree, a cloud, the smell of the wind, a leaf, or a small insect. Take a picture or draw the things you find along your way; try to describe the colors, the light, and the smells that characterize what you observe. The important thing is to stop and fully enjoy this moment of focus and awareness.

The Voice of Nature

The chirping of crickets, the crackling of a small campfire, the rustling of leaves in the wind, the twitter of a bird flying in the sky, the bubbling of a brook—these are only some examples of sounds we typically associate with being outdoors in an unspoiled environment, where we feel at ease with ourselves and others.

The effect that listening to natural sounds has on our psyche is well documented in a study conducted by the Brighton and Sussex Medical School that was published in *Scientific Reports* in 2017. Dr. Cassandra Gould and her team, in collaboration with the audiovisual artist Mark Ware, who specializes in audio recording and processing, subjected a group of volunteers to a series of recorded natural sounds interspersed with the typical sounds of a city. During the experiment, the brain activity of each volunteer was measured with an MRI and the activity of the nervous system was measured through heart rate. The results of the study led to the awareness that the default mode network, the "rest and digest" autonomic nervous system, changed configuration according to the sounds heard. When the participants were exposed to artificial sounds, brain activity indicated that the focus tended to close inward, thus facilitating the onset of symptoms common to conditions such as clinical depression, anxiety disorders, and post-traumatic stress disorder.

On the other hand, those who listened to natural sounds concentrated their attention on what was around them, appearing more awake and focused, while at the same time feeling relaxed. The sympathetic nervous system, which is responsible for the fight-or-flight reaction in dangerous or stressful situations, was at rest, and the parasympathetic nervous system, responsible for metabolism, recovery, and the development of the body's resources, was activated.

Immerse yourself for a moment in a garden, a park, or an outdoor space with some greenery. For this exercise, you need not be in a forest or in the middle of unspoiled nature. Stop and try to distinguish the sounds that characterize the natural environment around you. Close your eyes and enjoy the moment. In your journal, note the sounds you heard and the sensations you felt.

Nature's Population

Walking in the woods, we can find living creatures that are very visible, such as trees, animals, and insects; but under our feet, a myriad of invisible forms of life are proliferating and multiplying in the earth, such as tiny insects, fungal hyphae, and a boundless constellation of yeasts, bacteria, viruses, molds, and other microorganisms.

Being aware of this multitude of living entities leads us to reflect on the fact that knowing nature also means understanding—or at least intuiting—the profound interdependence between all these forms of life and the synergies they are able to generate between them.

This set of life forms is called biodiversity. The relationship between the set of living organisms and non-living matter—that is, between biotic and abiotic factors—constitutes a self-sufficient system in dynamic equilibrium known as the *ecosystem*. *Habitat* is defined as a place with the physical and environmental characteristics that allow a specific species to proliferate.

Therefore, an ecosystem can be made up of many living species and many habitats. When humans were limited to gathering what they needed from the land, before the advent of agriculture, they were well aware of the dynamics that governed a habitat and the forms of life that lived there. They knew the role of each species, including their own, in the network of interconnections that guaranteed an equilibrium that was constant over time.

But from the moment human beings jumped to the top of the food chain, not through gradual evolution but after sudden revolutionary events, they began to grow further and further removed from the natural context in which they lived. Modern contemporary man has completed the process of disconnecting with nature that began thousands of years ago; the time has now come to reverse course and reestablish our knowledge of the natural habitats whose balance we have destroyed through our constant abuse.

The next time you visit a city park or an unspoiled environment, try
to take a census of the trees, the animals, and the insects you find along
the way. Using a book of botany or a cellphone app that identifies plants
and animals, try to list the species you find and write them in your journal.
If you want, you can draw or take photos of what you see and take notes
on your experience. It will help you memorize something new each time.

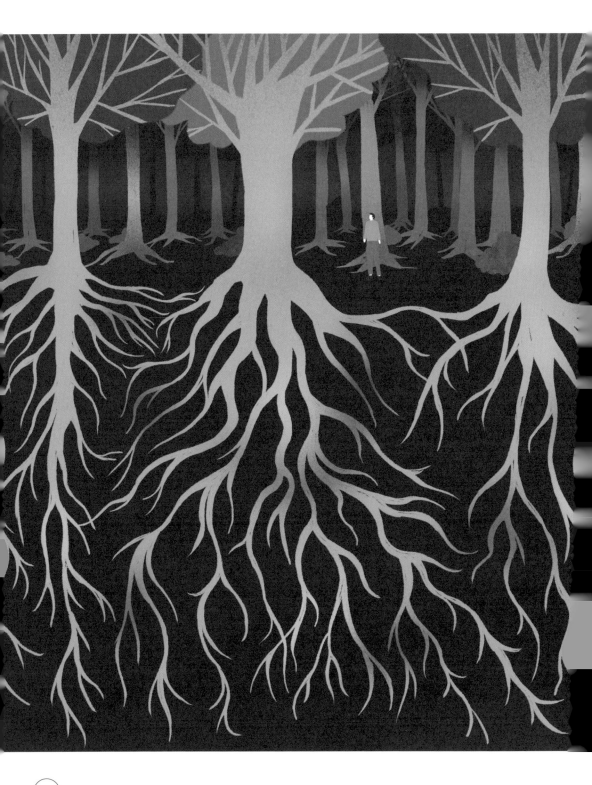

Getting into the Microcosm

Understanding that each thing in nature is connected and essential to a balance of life is one of the fundamental principles that we have to grasp in order to progress in the process of re-wilding. Each thing is connected to all the others, in terms of both cause and effect, and interdependent relationships.

For example, despite seeming like solitary, immobile, self-sufficient beings, trees, bushes, brambles, and shrubs have a very complex relationship to one another. Scientists have demonstrated that plant life is not static at all. On the contrary, plants communicate with each other, they exchange nourishment, and they even fight. They do this through a complex network of fungal tissues called *hyphae* that grow around and inside the roots. These networks are used by plants to perform a variety of operations and can extend for hundreds of kilometers. These communication networks, similar to the internet, have been called the "wood-wide web" by Suzanne Simard, a Canadian scientist and professor at the Faculty of Forestry of the University of British Columbia, who studies symbiotic forest networks.

Through the "wood-wide web", an adult tree can send nourishment to young trees of the same species growing around it, like a mother nursing her young, or it can distribute its residual resources to its neighbors if it is dying. Additionally, if a plant is attacked by a parasite, it can let the plants around it know by sending a chemical signal that allows the other plants to organize their defenses. Even the "wood-wide web" has a dark side; it can be used for purposes that are not exactly pacific. In fact, a plant can take resources and nourishment away from its competitors in a predatory act, or it can emit toxic substances or herbicides to the network in order to conquer a territory claimed by more than one species.

Go to the woods and start walking among the trees. Try to visualize an underground network of microfilaments that connect the plants you see. Try to imagine the forest itself as one complex organism, rather than a sum of plants that are isolated and do not communicate with each other.

The Scent of Nature

Why are many cosmetics enriched with fragrances that reproduce the scents emanated by flowers, trees, and other plants? For the same reason that walking in a forest gives us a sense of well-being, relaxation, and being in contact with nature. It is precisely because of the close relationship between natural scents and the positive mental response they create.

Recent studies reveal that what we call a woodsy scent has a strong regenerating, balancing, and healing power because of the high concentration of monoterpenes in the forest air. These organic, aromatic substances are produced by plants, fungi, bacteria, and even some insects. Together with the essential oils of the woody parts of larger plants, they are responsible for the scents we perceive when we visit a forest. Absorbing monoterpenes through our skin and our mucous membranes has a positive effect on our bodies and our minds. Walking in beech forests, in birch woods, or among lush oaks and trees with large leaves that easily release those substances into the air, increases the positive effect on our health and our mood.

Visiting these forests often, practicing forest bathing—or, as Tomohide Akiyama, Japan's Minister of Agriculture, christened it in the 1980s, *shinrin-yoku*, or "bathing in the forest"—can be important in improving many aspects of our lives.

Go into a forest and begin walking among the trees. Try to identify the holly oaks, the beech trees, the oaks, the birches, and the conifers. Breathe slowly and deeply, focusing on the characteristics of the scents you smell and the effect they have on your body and mind. Make a note in your journal of the paths you have taken and the sensations you have experienced while walking in these areas, in order to create an archive of the possible forest-bathing paths you have at your disposal.

A BATH
IN THE FOREST

The fundamental principle at the base of the Japanese therapy *shinrin-yoku*, or forest bathing, is the idea that spending time in the woods brings some surprising health benefits. In a series of studies published in 2007 in the *International Journal of Immunopathology and Pharmacology*, a team of Japanese scientists discovered that spending a few hours in environments such as forests, parks, or other areas with a dense tree population increases immune response. Scientifically measured benefits included lower concentrations of cortisol, the hormone produced in conjunction with stress, anger, and anxiety; lower heart rate and blood pressure; and the consequent benefits in the treatment of many physical and psychological ailments. The practice of forest bathing is spreading rapidly, with sessions being organized all over the world.

The Life of Giants

Sometimes when we go for a walk in the woods, it seems like we have gone back to a comfortable place filled with memories; but to feel truly at home and reestablish a deep relationship with the environment, we need to have a better knowledge of the trees that grow there, including their names and characteristics. I use *PlantNet*, an app that provides the scientific name and other details about the species with a photograph; but the most fundamental thing we can do to help us learn and memorize is to observe attentively.

When we find ourselves in front of a tree that is new to us, let's begin by focusing on the leaves and their shape, color, outline, and the way they connect to the branches. Let's pick one with a stem and tape it to a page in the journal, and describe it using simple words. Next, let's look at the bark, which can have a variety of colors and textures. This part of the tree is always unique, as though it were the plant's fingerprint, and it often allows us to partially reconstruct its history, through scars or other signs. Try placing a page from your journal over the bark and rubbing it with dry soil, a wax crayon, colored chalk, or anything else you can use to make an impression. Take a few steps back, look at the outline of the tree in its entirety, and make a sketch of it in your journal. Each species has its own specific shape that defines its identity. For example, consider the cypress or the spruce. We have known how to recognize some trees by their shape since we were children. Finally, let's try to identify the type of seeds, fruits, buds, or flowers the tree produces, since they will be very important details to draw in order to finish our description of the tree.

Each time a tree catches your attention, write a detailed description in your journal. As time goes by, you will collect a myriad of species and increase your knowledge of the green giants that grow around us.

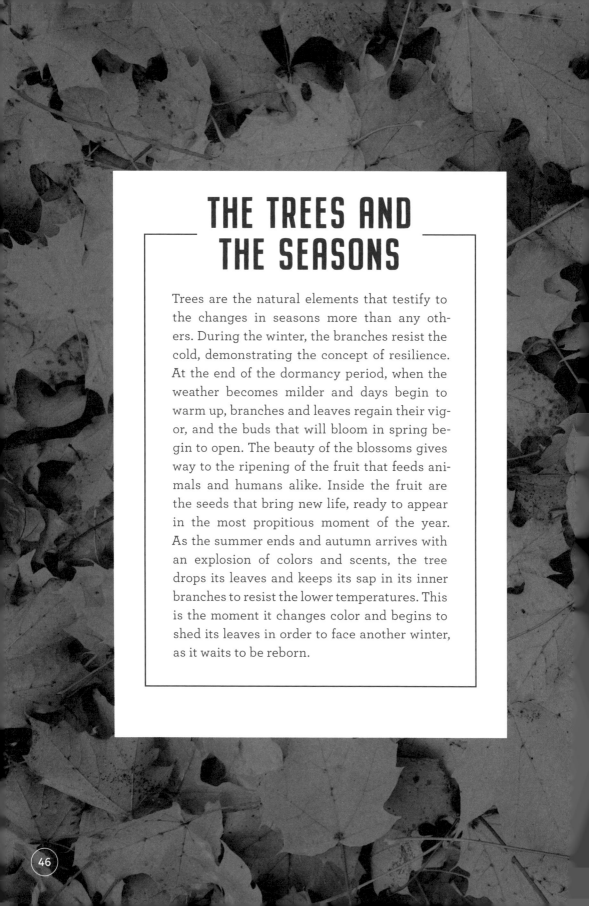

THE TREES AND THE SEASONS

Trees are the natural elements that testify to the changes in seasons more than any others. During the winter, the branches resist the cold, demonstrating the concept of resilience. At the end of the dormancy period, when the weather becomes milder and days begin to warm up, branches and leaves regain their vigor, and the buds that will bloom in spring begin to open. The beauty of the blossoms gives way to the ripening of the fruit that feeds animals and humans alike. Inside the fruit are the seeds that bring new life, ready to appear in the most propitious moment of the year. As the summer ends and autumn arrives with an explosion of colors and scents, the tree drops its leaves and keeps its sap in its inner branches to resist the lower temperatures. This is the moment it changes color and begins to shed its leaves in order to face another winter, as it waits to be reborn.

Chapter 2

FEELING NATURE

Rights of Nature

....

From the time the Soviet Union launched Sputnik, the first man-made satellite, into space in 1957, an increasing number of artificial objects has been put into space every year to meet our needs for telecommunications, research, experimentation, and military defenses. Since 2010, the frequency with which these launches take place has risen drastically, reaching 146 launches in 2021 and beating the record set in 1967 of 136.

The aerospace company SpaceX alone has put fifty-one Starlink satellites into orbit, thus contributing to the dense cloud of electronic devices that chase each other around Earth and are destined to fall back to Earth as space junk in a few years. It has become evident that even a remote space like the earth's orbit is now at risk of filling up with high-tech garbage, once again demonstrating that, for humans, conquering a natural space means exploiting it until it is destroyed.

Our species also takes this approach to what it needs for our survival or well-being. Industries are destroying entire habitats, including forests and oceans, making the environmental impact of production and distribution unsustainable.

This concept of nature as a sum of endless reserves at the service of humans is a sad confirmation that man's scientific and cultural progress seems inversely proportional to his capacity to feel like part of nature. If this were not the case, the concept of evolution would be closely tied to environmental protection, the safeguarding of plant species, of animals, of the land, and of air quality.

Theoretically, the bond between human rights and environmental protection was established in 1972, at the United Nations Conference on the Human Environment in Stockholm, where the Stockholm *Declaration and Action Plan for the Human Environment* was adopted.

Principle 1 of the declaration states: "Man has the fundamental right to freedom, equality and adequate conditions of life, in an environment of quality that permits a life of dignity and well-being, and he bears a solemn responsibility to protect and improve the environment for present and future generations." This recognition is important in that it identifies an environmental component in the protection of human rights, which then becomes a part of the existing obligations that states must respect, protect and realize.

So, if humans have succeeded in defining their right to protect their environment for future generations, why are they unable to stop destroying the planet and the space surrounding it? This contradictory behavior gives rise to the idea that two different categories of human beings exist: those who understand the importance of living in an environment that is intact and healthy, and those who give less importance to nature than to profit, scientific research, or going beyond human and technological limits for the sake of doing so. To become a part of the category that cares about the planet and environmental protection, you only need to study, to learn about, to become closer to, and to observe the environment, the animals, and geology, and take the time to appreciate them. One small but significant step would be to simply spend more time outdoors, in contact with the real world, rather than staying purposely and sadly isolated from the world that surrounds you.

The journey toward reconnection with nature continues.

Cultivating Gratitude

To truly love and respect nature requires empathy, the ability to put oneself in someone else's shoes and to understand their mental and behavioral processes; but nature is a complex subject, made of inorganic material and billions of species of interdependent beings: flora, fauna, bacteria, fungi, viruses, and anything we define as living beings. This is why we need to extend our concept of empathy. It must include the ability to perceive and experience emotions in response to the phenomena that govern the functions of organic and inorganic subjects in nature and the relationships that bind them.

Learning to recognize and accept these emotions is a fundamental part of growing and reestablishing an authentic relationship with nature, even if these emotions may not always be positive or linked to "good" events.

Nature is also made up of phenomena that we regard as unjust or "bad," such as earthquakes, tornadoes, killings, viruses, fires, and so on; but nature is neutral, it is neither for nor against humans. We are simply one of the elements that comprise it, and certainly not the central key of its existence, regardless of what we are used to thinking.

Feeling empathetic with nature means accepting its beauty along with the harshness of its power: both the joy and the fear of being in a pristine setting mean experiencing life but also experiencing death.

How do you cultivate *gratitude*? The effect and primary cause of gratitude is the mind's disposition to find positive elements in our daily lives. It is not just about thanking those who help us; rather, it is a real feeling stemming from the empathy we feel toward others and our self-awareness. The only way to cultivate gratitude is to override your ego and put yourself in a position to listen to and feel your neighbors, whether they be people, animals, or plants. Feeling ourselves a part of a whole, neither above nor separate from nature, is the key step in generating gratitude and in living our role on this planet in communion with the rest of the species that share it with us.

Imagine your life as something that happens in unison with
all the other beings present on the planet and in the universe.
Let your gratitude bloom because you are experiencing
existence as a part of this complex, interdependent,
and endless system called nature.

Going Out in the Rain

Rain plays a fundamental role in the water cycle. The water that evaporates from the oceans condenses in the clouds and falls back to earth, returning to the oceans in streams, lakes, rivers, and underground aquifers to repeat the cycle again. As the water becomes available to the biosphere, it allows the flora and fauna to develop, thus improving the planet's livability.

There is no need to run for shelter when a sudden downpour occurs. Slow your pace and look up into the sky to welcome this common but enchanting phenomenon.

Some cultures seem to be less affected by the weather, and treat walking in the rain as completely normal. In Norway, there is a proverb: *"Det finnes ikke dårlig vær, bare dårlige klær,"* which can be translated as "There is no such thing as bad weather, only bad clothes." A pair of waterproof pants and a jacket will keep you dry and warm, and you can enjoy the benefits of walking in the pouring rain without risking your health.

What are the benefits of being out in the rain? There are many. Enjoying a moment of peace and serenity by yourself or in a small group, even in a city park, is truly priceless. Air quality improves because raindrops have the ability to attract hundreds of particles of pollutants such as soot, sulfates, and bacteria before they hit the ground. In addition, when the drops touch the ground, they release what we call petrichor, the smell of the rain, which has a deeply calming effect on the mind. Finally, when we take regular walks in the rain, we learn to relinquish control and become more confident and courageous.

When it rains, leave your car and your umbrella at home. Put on a waterproof jacket and pants, go outside, enjoy the rain, and reflect!

THE RAIN

In the scientific language of meteorology, rainfall is measured in millimeters (mm); 1 mm (0.039 in) of rain is equivalent to 1 liter (0.264 US gal) of water falling on an area of 1 m^2 (10.76 sq. ft). The amount of rain that falls annually in a certain area of the planet, together with the temperature, determines what kind of climate the area has. One serious consequence of climate change is the great intensity of rains that fall in a brief period of time. These storms are called cloudbursts.

Normally, part of the rain that falls from the clouds does not reach the ground. It evaporates into the air as it descends, particularly if the air it passes through is warm or dry. Small raindrops are almost round, ones that are bigger (2 to 15 mm in diameter) are flatter, like a loaf of bread, and those that are even bigger are concave and shaped like a parachute, slowing down their descent. On average, the drops are 1 to 2 mm in diameter. The largest drops were recorded in Brazil and in the Marshall Islands in 2004; they measured over 1 cm (0.39 in) in diameter.

Let's Sow Seeds

The time has come to plant a little garden that will allow us to observe how plants grow and to learn about their development cycle, from planting to harvesting. I will also allow us to enjoy a firsthand look at the growth and development phases of the plants we might put on our table. Getting your hands in the dirt to take care of plants and flowers also improves your mood. It relaxes your mind and your body and teaches you to be responsible for other living creatures. These aspects make planting and caring for plants an ideal activity for children, but even as adults, we can learn a lesson from it.

It makes no difference whether the space we have available is a terrace, a windowsill, or a garden. Get a large pot or a series of smaller pots, and a bag of soil for plants. Both are easy to find in your supermarket or in a greenhouse or nursery. When you buy fertilizers, soil, insecticides, and fungicides, opt for organic, natural products. Make sure they have a label certifying that they are "approved for organic farming." Next, we need to choose the seeds we want to grow. Obviously, we should respect the correct sowing and germination cycles. Each plant has its own calendar that you can learn about on the internet, so you can begin your garden at any time. A long time ago, I planted an acorn from an oak tree. It sprouted and became a small tree. Now it is big enough to transplant in the yard, where it will become as much a member of the family as a cat or dog.

When you plant your garden, take notes in your journal about the important steps: when you sow, how often you irrigate, when the first sprouts come up, and the various growth phases. Keeping track of your plants' progress is important for observing the workings of nature and the cyclicity of the seasons, and for learning from any errors you might make.

Getting the Messages

Along the path of re-wilding, it is fundamental to keep in mind that nature sends an infinity of messages. These messages can help us decipher a lot of information that we will find useful in our lives, and it is our duty to try to understand them. The information often is symbolic; it invites us to look for something deeply authentic in ourselves.

Keep an open mind about the messages held in the natural environments you visit—they are everywhere. One example that is particularly meaningful for me happened during a long walk in Valmalenco, in the Alps in central Italy. I came upon a larch that had fallen toward the valley, onto a path. The scene was rather dramatic, with the powerful tree showing its roots, which were surprisingly light-colored despite the dark, rocky soil hanging from them. They were mighty but useless, defeated. The tree was still alive, but the fall was fatal, there was no doubt about it. It was an impressive sight to see; a colossal tree struck down by a mysterious force, perhaps by its own enormity, which had suddenly become unsustainable. Seeing that tree taught me many powerful lessons about nature, reality, and the eternal laws that govern them. The beauty of these messages is that they are true for all forms of life, including us humans. They make us aware that we are already connected to nature; we only need to be less distracted.

Look for the messages that nature is sending you. Reflect on the fact that it communicates with symbols that are everywhere. During your excursions, keep your eyes open, observe, and take note in your journal of any thoughts the place you are visiting suggests.

Hunting for Jewels

When our primitive ancestors began exploring the world, they immediately began collecting and preserving amulets of various kinds: bones, stones, horns, claws, teeth, feathers, and anything else that had a strong symbolic power capable of bringing protection and good luck.

Even today, we still have the habit of entrusting our good luck or protection to an object. For example, think about how lucky we feel when we find a four-leaf clover, or the way we choose our clothes for an important job interview, or the ring we never take off because it represents the love of another person, or the medal we wear around our neck every day as protection. All of these can be considered amulets, and at this point, we know that magic is alive and thriving in modern society today.

As you are taking a walk, many objects will get your attention: acorns and other seeds, small crystals, feathers, stones, and many other things. If they transmit positive feelings to you, you can take them and adopt them as amulets, and implant the power of your desires in them. The so-called hag stone is a good example of an amulet. These stones have holes in them that are natural, not man-made, and they have been worn as pendants for thousands of years. Some people even believe that they are true portals through which you can get or ward off energy, and some think that they can bring good luck or ward off bad luck, and attract wealth or protect you from poverty. Collect the objects you find in a cloth sack: you can keep them in your pocket and admire them at any time of the day.

On your next walk, look for stones that inspire good intentions in you: cones, feathers, stones, crystals, and small pieces of wood that somehow inspire joy, enchantment, protection, confidence. Collect these objects and note the time and place you found them in your journal. Describe what you felt when you collected them, and what they mean to you. Once you get home, clean them and put them with care into a small bag that you can take with you whenever you want.

THE NEANDERTHAL'S LAST NECKLACE

In the cave of Cova Foradada in Calafell, a Spanish village in Catalonia a few kilometers south of Barcelona, archeologists discovered the carved phalanx of an eagle talon made by a Neanderthal man or woman dating back to about 40,000 years ago. According to researchers, Neanderthals in that period came into contact with *Homo sapiens,* who were spreading from the Middle East and from Northern Africa into Southern Europe. It was nicknamed "the Neanderthal's last necklace" because it is one of the last artifacts they made before becoming extinct.

Marks on the amulet led researchers to believe that it was worn as a pendant on a necklace, probably to indicate the status of the person wearing it, and may have had the purpose of sending a specific message to the community. The Iberian eagle, the raptor the talon belonged to, was very difficult to catch, so this ornamental object may have been a sign of particular hunting skills, intelligence, or strength. This important find also demonstrated that the Neanderthals were skilled artisans, capable of formulating complex, abstract thoughts and of creating symbols and objects of art.

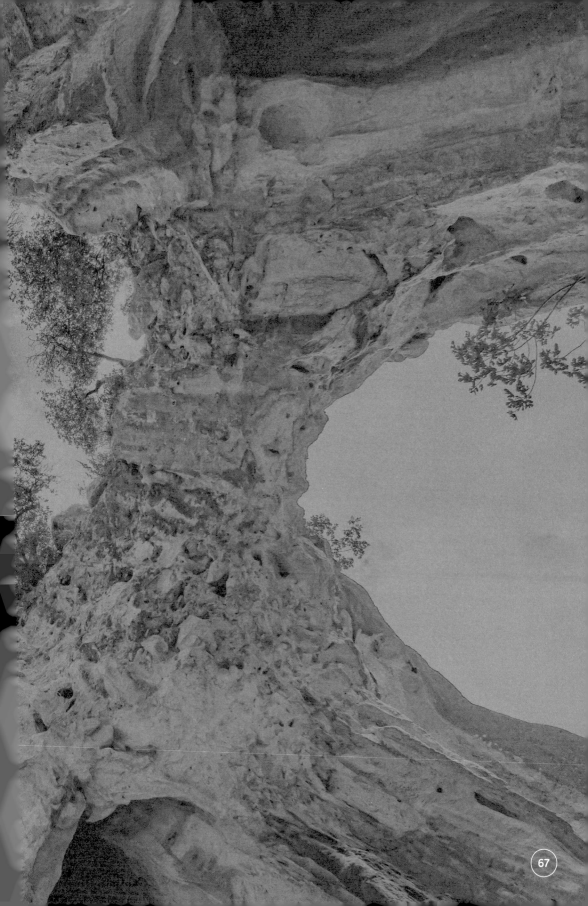

Using Your Journal to Record

Our travel journal can become a sketchbook where we describe and reproduce the shapes and colors of plant species—herbs, flowers, bushes, fruit, seeds, trees—and other natural elements that catch our attention. To document by sketching means we have to focus on the general aspect of a natural element and on the way it works, an unbeatable way to learn.

Let's begin by gathering something that catches our attention, such as a flower, a leaf, a pinecone, an acorn, or an herb. Look at it very carefully, following its outline with your eyes, noting small details, its shades of color, and the consistency of its surface. Begin your drawing by outlining the object with a hard lead pencil, and then try to reproduce its general size and proportions. Take your time on the more complex parts, such as intersections or geometric lines that we find within the shapes. Then go over the defined lines with a softer pencil and embellish the sketch with the smallest details such as the flower stems, the veins of the leaves, and so on. Finally, color your drawing, choosing the pastels that are closest to the color you have observed in nature. Remember, no one is able to make a perfect drawing on the first try; the beauty of this practice is also to chart our technical progress over time. You will discover that drawing is an endless source of serenity and relaxation, and that it can bring you the same benefits meditation does. Over time, your willpower will grow stronger, which will allow you to develop your drawing skills as well as many other aspects of your life that require dedication and practice over a long period of time.

For this practice, you will need a journal, pencils of varying hardness and colors, and pastels. When your sketch is complete, look for the scientific and common names of the element that you have drawn. This will help you to transform your journal into an herbarium, and you can learn to recognize plants and other objects in nature as you page through the drawings you have made over time.

Using Your Journal to Map

Exploration—from the Latin word *explorare,* meaning to observe, examine, search—is part of our innate instinct to discover and know the territory that surrounds us. This instinct probably arose from our prehistoric ancestors' need to scour the land in search of food; but the oldest recognized map has to do with the sky, not the land. On the walls of the Lascaux caves in France, a prehistoric sky map dating to around 16,500 BC was discovered. In this map of the night sky, Vega, Deneb, Altair, and the Pleiades are recognizable.

Exploration and mapping are two closely tied concepts. We have never stopped creating maps, from the time of those first Paleolithic sketches until today, when satellites provide us with photographic documentation of every corner of our planet. To map our natural environment, however, we must know it in depth and in its true essence to be able to share important information with our community. This information includes the types of vegetation present, the location of the plants, the availability of edible fruit and berries, details regarding the terrain, and the presence of water sources, trees, animal dens, paths, reference points, and dangers.

Each time you visit a territory you want to map, orient yourself with a compass. In your journal, note the direction you are walking. Try to draw lines that are proportional to the time it takes to complete each tract at a normal pace, and keep north at the top of your page. When you come across something that catches your attention—a thousand-year-old tree, a fence, the stones of a house in ruins, a great bramble of blackberries, or any other detail—draw it. It could be useful to orient yourself when you come walking in the area in the future.

Orientation

Leaving a path and going into unknown territory can be a great way to enjoy one of those moments of liberty that we often deny ourselves, a moment in which we can get lost and then rediscover our way back to a safe place. The following are some important elements to orient yourself and to understand where the cardinal directions lie. The first thing to consider is that, even though the exact points vary with the seasons, the sun rises in the east and sets in the west. In the Northern Hemisphere, a shadow projected onto the ground at around noon will always face north, while in the Southern Hemisphere it will face south.

In the Northern Hemisphere at night, when the stars are visible, you can look for the North Star, a dim star in the Little Dipper that is always directly to the north. In the Southern Hemisphere, instead, you can look for the Southern Cross, a constellation made of five stars. An imaginary line that runs vertically through the stars points south.

There are a number of ways to use the territory for orientation. Remember that the northern face of a tree trunk is generally covered in moss, due to increased moisture there; on the stumps of cut trees, growth rings are wider on the southern side, the same side where foliage is thicker and to which blossoms are oriented; the sun melts the snow faster on southern-facing terrain; moss grows on the northern-facing sides of rocks where there is more moisture in the underbrush, and the southern-facing sides of rocks are cleaner and drier.

Look for signals that allow you to get your bearings next time you explore a natural territory. After you have found the north, using a compass if necessary, look around you for signs of adaptation in the natural elements there, such as moss, moisture, plant and leaf density, and so on.

ORIENTEERING

Orienteering is a competitive recreational sport that allows us to explore a territory with awareness, played prevalently outdoors in contact with nature. It promotes respect for the environment, stimulates a spirit of independence, initiative, and collaboration, and makes recreational use of the forests and natural environments in which it takes place. Orienteering requires that participants be able to interpret maps, read scale and altitude variations, and use a compass to identify the correct path in relation to the map.

Orienteering is a time trial that takes place in diverse terrain. Using a compass and a topographical map, competitors must complete a path (indicated in red on the map) and reach the finish line in the shortest possible time. A triangle indicates the starting line, and two concentric circles indicate the finish line. Along their route, competitors must pass through a series of progressively numbered control points, called lanterns, in the correct order, and punch the race cards they received at the starting line. The first competitor or team to reach the finish line with all the control cards punched in the correct order wins.

On Your Tiptoes

In 2007, researchers from the Zoological Institute of the University of Berne carried out a study that showed that skiers, snowboarders, and excursionists could have a negative impact on the already difficult existence of wild animals, particularly in winter or during their reproductive season. In fact, for many animals who do not hibernate, particularly in mid- and high-mountain environments, very low temperatures and the scarcity of food make survival extremely difficult.

Animals perceive human presence in their territory as a serious danger and adopt defensive behavior such as flight, which burns a great amount of energy. Abandoning their burrows and dens causes them serious stress that impacts their health. A study of the impact of excursionists and skiers on species like the black grouse (*Lyrurus tetrix*) shows that these animals, who take refuge in hidden shelters during the winter, reduce their activities to a minimum to save as much energy as possible, and that loud voices, sudden movements, and unexpected noises can cause panic and endanger their lives. The research team monitored levels of corticosterone, a stress-related hormone, in the species involved in the study. They found that animals living in areas visited by humans had a 20% higher concentration of this hormone than those living where there was no human presence. From now on, let's always remember how important it is to take care of the plants, trees, and animals that populate a natural environment, and that to do so, we must avoid making too much noise when we are out in nature.

When you explore a natural environment, particularly in winter, be careful of the amount of noise you make. Try to keep your voice down and avoid making sudden, disturbing noises. Try to minimize the impact of your presence by turning off the ringer on your cell phone and trying not to yell or talk loudly, clap your hands, drop heavy objects, and so on.

Taking Note of Tracks

The forests, the mountains, and the prairies are brimming with life, just like any natural environment; and although we are not always aware of animals hiding in the bushes or in the treetops, we can find signs of their presence in the tracks they leave on the ground.

Snow, mud, sand, and generally any soft terrain is ideal for gathering information about the animals that live in the area we are exploring. The first thing to note when we see footprints, other than their shape, is the gait they suggest. A zigzag gait is the sign of a "perfect walker." Deer, moose, foxes, and lynxes all walk carefully this way, to save energy. The back paw lands precisely where the front paw has just left a print. On the other hand, tracks left when the back paw does not come down close to the print left by the front paw will leave four prints in a so-called waddling track pattern, a gait typical of bears, beavers, and groundhogs. When we see tracks with two parallel prints, the gait is called a bounding track pattern, typical of frogs or otters. Finally, if the prints of the back paws are outside and a bit ahead of the front paws, the gait is called a galloping track pattern, left by horses, mice, rabbits, and squirrels.

To identify the weight of the animal, remember that the heavier the animal, the deeper its print, and the distance between two aligned prints, for example of the front left and front right paws, can help estimate the animal's size.

The next time you are walking and you find a paw print, observe it closely, try to draw it in your journal, and take note of its characteristics. Mark the spot where you found it on a map if you are using one or if you are creating one in your journal. When you get home, try to discover the animal's identity based on the shape of the print and look for information in books or online to get to know the animals that populate the area you explored.

THE WOLF

The wolf (*Canis lupus*) is a carnivorous mammal that belongs to the Canidae family. It is very adaptable, elusive, fast, and resistant. It can run over 31 miles (50 km) in a night and has senses that are much more highly developed than those of a dog. Its excellent vision and hearing are used for two of the most important activities of its life: interspecies communication, and hunting. However, its most acute sense is undoubtedly its sense of smell, which governs the major functions of its life cycle: reproduction, inter-individual communication, and food finding.

The wolf was initially one of the most diffuse mammals on the Earth, living in a habitat that included North America, Europe, and Asia. Conflict created mainly in relation to cattle breeding caused the wolf to disappear from most of central and northern Europe. Since the middle of the twentieth century, ecological and social factors have made it possible for the wolf to expand once again into a wide variety of ecosystems, from the Arctic tundra to the Arabian Desert and on the American and Eurasian continents. Its ability to survive in a variety of environments, feeding on every available food source, and its ability to move even in unfavorable habitats, have been fundamental in the wolf's recovery. There are an estimated 300,000 wolves in the world today.

Chapter 3

FEEDING YOURSELF WITH NATURE

Exploring to Survive

....

We use the Latin term *Homo sapiens*, or "wise man," to define modern humans as they were classified in 1758 by Carl Linnaeus (Carl von Linné) in his book *Systema Naturae.* For the first time, this publication presented the current scientific nomenclature for classifying all living things according to *genus* followed by *species.* Our species celebrated itself with the adjective *sapiens* as part of the genus *Homo* in direct descent from Australopithecus and from *Homo habilis*, the first hominid who built stone tools.

Scientists agree that our species appeared about two hundred thousand years ago near the Zambezi River, in what is now northern Botswana. The morphological and physical features of the *sapiens*, including brain size and the skeletal proportions between arms, legs, and skull, were already the same as those that Leonardo da Vinci represented in his famous design, the *Vitruvian Man.* He wanted to demonstrate how the human figure could be harmoniously inscribed in the two "perfect" figures of the circle, which symbolizes Heaven—the divine perfection, and the square, which symbolizes Earth.

The first *sapiens* that began to spread in Africa, Europe, and the rest of the world were primarily hunters of small animals and gatherers of herbs, roots, fruits, berries, mushrooms, and anything edible they found in the territories where they wandered, with no permanent dwellings. Paleoanthropologists hypothesize that our ancestors were experts at recognizing the hundreds of edible or toxic wild species that grew around them, even giving them names. The constant need to find sources of subsistence made it necessary for *Homo sapiens* to accumulate knowledge that would allow them to recognize wild foods, and to establish a strong connection to nature that would allow them to understand the mechanisms that made food available.

This close relationship between necessity and knowledge also shaped our senses and our physical structure. For example, our pre-historic ancestors could taste different types of bitterness, some of which were associated with toxins and poisons. Today, we have almost completely lost this ability because our tongues are no longer trained to assess possible dangers from poisoning. We have also lost much of the wealth of knowledge that our ancestors handed down about recognizing and collecting edible species. After all, food is now readily available on supermarket shelves, so we no longer need to know what to gather from the natural environment and when to do it.

About ten thousand years ago, we began selecting seeds from species that were more resistant to bacteria and weather. This was the advent of agriculture. This shift revolutionized the lifestyle of our ancestors, who gradually abandoned nomadism to tend their fields and wait for crops. Agriculture then laid the foundations of medieval and later modern society, of trade, and of the control of land and resources, which reached its zenith with the advent of industry and the post-industrial era. Humans progressively abandoned the countryside, the mountains, the forests, and even their cultivated fields, moving to urban settlements and entrusting their subsistence to the industry of food production and distribution. In just a few generations, humans lost the ability to interact with wild nature and isolated themselves from it completely. They began exploiting resources without understanding the dangers of the consequent imbalance they were creating in ecosystems.

The results of this ill-considered plundering of natural resources is clearly evident: global warming, glacial melting, climate change, groundwater pollution, and the disappearance of biodiversity.

The time has come to re-appropriate our knowledge of wild food gathering—the only effective way for us to truly understand the importance of preserving the natural environment for present and future generations.

Let's start by viewing our surroundings through the eyes of a forager.

Becoming a Forager!

The figure of the forager, a gatherer of ingredients growing in the wild, is somewhere between that of the explorer and the scientist, someone who is able to establish a direct relationship with nature as its observer and protector. To become a forager of wild-growing food, we have to acquire the abilities and knowledge needed to explore a natural environment, and to identify and correctly collect edible species of plants.

There are roots with unexpected flavors, leaves rich in varied aromas, herbs that bring character to a recipe. To be a forager requires a profound knowledge of the wild ingredients available in the territory we are exploring. We must be careful to gather only those species we can eat and to recognize those that are toxic. Get yourself a book about botany or a manual for foraging to help you begin to distinguish the most common species of plants that grow around you, even in the parks of your city.

A forager also needs to know which period is right for foraging a specific plant. For example, in the northern temperate zones in January, you can find chickweed, sorrel, and meadow chervil; in April, wild garlic; in June, wild chamomile, honeysuckle, and elderflower; in September, rosehip berries; and in November, hazelnuts, blackthorn, and walnuts.

Foragers are also explorers and observers of the territory and its climate, witnesses and guardians of the health conditions of the habitats they explore. It is common to witness such bizarre phenomena as anomalous blossoms in the middle of winter or late spring frosts that disrupt the normal development cycles of plants, which are a sign of climate anomalies.

Each time you get ready for an excursion, find out about the wild herbs you expect to find in the territory you plan to explore. Make a list of the names of the species that are common in the habitat you are about to discover, and try to memorize the shape of the leaves, flowers, roots, and aspect of each one so you can recognize them during your walk.

THE RULES OF FORAGING

There are some basic rules that a real forager must follow carefully:

- never gather something without knowing for certain what it is and that it is edible;
- never leave signs of your presence behind you, and try to leave our natural wealth intact;
- give the plants you gather the possibility to continue to reproduce, cutting only the upper part and leaving the roots;
- forage in public lands that are not contaminated by groundwater, air, or water pollution;
- forage only what you really need, without creating waste, and always leave an ample amount of what you are foraging for others;
- share your knowledge and never stop studying and analyzing;
- never harm the trees by removing bark, and do not extract sap without knowing how to do it correctly;
- get informed about the protected species present in the area you are exploring, because all bans against foraging must be rigorously respected.

Making an Herbarium

An herbarium is a book that holds a collection of plants that are dried, glued to a page, and classified, accompanied by information including their scientific names, where and when they were gathered, the type of terrain they were growing in and at what altitude, along with any other details that help describe them.

Creating an herbarium in the pages of your journal can be a good way to recognize the edible plants you have already foraged, observed, and studied.

Each time you find a plant species that you think is edible but that you have not yet catalogued, you can pick it, unless it is a protected species.

Try to keep as many as possible of the plant's parts intact, including its roots. If you find berries, try to cut the small stem they are growing on so that you can closely observe the plant's leaves, buds, and any other useful detail. There is no need to forage too many species all at once, since it is best to find the time and resources to carry out a complete analysis of each one. When you are sure that you have identified the type of plant and its edibility, glue it to a page in your journal or draw it and color it, trying to reproduce how the leaves grow on its stem, its shape, the color of its flowers, and so on. Complete the page by writing the common and scientific names of the species, its habitat, and the time of year it can be foraged. You can complete the information with a description of the way it tastes and to which recipe it would add flavor.

Use the pages of your journal to catalogue the edible plant species you find during your explorations. These pages do not need to be one after the other; use the first free page available.

THE DIOSCORIDES HERBARIUM

The first known herbarium was made by Dioscorides of Anarzabus. A Greek physician and botanist from Cilicia, he arrived in Nero's Rome in the first century AD, where he wrote his most important work, *De materia medica*. The oldest copy of the illustrated volume is the Vienna Dioscorides, with four hundred miniatures and more than six hundred types of plants with their therapeutic properties. The book is now held among the manuscripts of the Austrian National Library in Vienna.

According to legend, the work was given to Anicia Juliana by the people of Constantinople around 512 AD to thank her for building a Christian church. There is also a Naples Dioscorides, held at the National Library of Naples. This herbarium is composed of 170 pages illustrated with splendid colored miniatures of known medicinal plants, accompanied by a written comment to describe each single plant, its habitat, and its therapeutic application.

The Forager's Equipment

Having the right equipment and tools can be a great help when you decide to look for wild food on your excursions. In any case, it is always a good idea to take what you might need to gather and transport wild food, should you find some along the way.

The first thing to put in the pocket of your backpack is a pair of scissors and a pocketknife. These two instruments are fundamental for picking the part of the plant that you want without ruining the rest. With the scissors, you can make a clean cut; but you should also learn to use your pocketknife because, in the long run, it will become a more versatile tool. Remember to bring a small linen sack that you can fold so it takes up as little space as possible in your backpack. This fabric will keep the plants fresh from the time you pick them until you use them in the kitchen. Gloves are also fundamental if you want to pick berries from thorny bushes or stinging plants. Remember to bring your herbarium as well, and, if you can, a pocket-sized botany manual that will help you identify plants, fruits, and other edible wild food.

Before you set off on your expedition, organize your tools in your backpack so they will be ready if you find any wild food. Take note in your journal and on your walking map of the locations that were richest in fruit, berries, herbs, and other foods. This will help you remember where to find the wild ingredients that you need in the future.

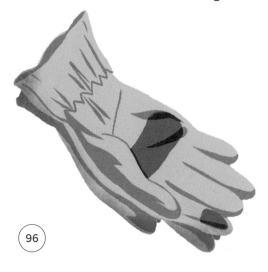

Wild Fruit

The small wild fruits you find when you are walking in the forest or in the countryside have a flavor that is decided and unusual, much stronger than the fruit you buy at the supermarket or fruit vendor. Observe the fruits you will find during your excursions and add them to your herbarium, distinguishing the species that are edible and that you like from those that are toxic and that you must avoid.

If you look carefully around you as you walk along country roads or in the woods during the summer or autumn, you can find some fruit to enjoy. Before you leave, get informed about which wild fruit species grow in the area you are going to explore.

Some are more easily recognizable than others are, such as raspberries, blueberries, or chestnuts, but there are many other lesser-known species for you to discover on your expeditions. On the internet or in a botany manual, you can find out how to recognize the strawberry tree (*Arbutus unedo*), the common barberry (*Berberis vulgaris*), the Cornelian cherry (*Cornus mas*), common juniper (*Juniperus communis*), white mulberry (*Morus alba*), blackthorn (*Prunus spinosa*), elm-leaf blackberry (*Rubus ulmifolius*), and black elder (*Sambucus nigra*). Taste the fruit of each plant, and pick a plant to include in your journal, draw it, and describe its characteristics—but be careful! It is vitally important to recognize and avoid the many fruits that are dangerous for your health.

> **Distinguishing the fruits you can eat from those you have to avoid means getting to know the enormous variety of wild fruit available. If you find wild fruit as you are walking, try to draw its shape, proportions, and colors with as much precision as possible so that you can recognize it in the future. Catalogue the species that are not edible as well, drawing them and describing them carefully so you can avoid them in the future.**

Wild Herbs

Foraging gives you the possibility of adding hundreds of kinds of wild herbs to your recipes to make extraordinary dishes. Some herbs taste fresh, some citrusy, some spicy, and so on. The combinations of flavors and aromas are infinite, and knowing how to use these ingredients can help enrich your diet with healthy, free food.

Recognizing the most common spontaneous plants is very important; I suggest you study the list below, since it is the base you can use to begin building your herbarium of edible plants.

The common dandelion (*Taraxacum officinale*) has a tough root and a classic, intense yellow flower with long petals that becomes a fuzzy seed head, called a pappus, when it finishes blooming. Its oblong leaves begin directly at the root, and its stem is hollow. It is very widespread and grows in open spaces. Both its leaves and its flowers are edible.

Borage (*Borago officinalis*) has a big blue star-shaped flower with radial petals and a fuzzy stem. It is an invasive species that grows in full sunlight. It can be picked in the summer and is part of the traditional cuisine in many parts of Europe.

The common nettle plant (*Urtica dioica*) is a stinging plant with irregular serrated leaves and grayish flowers. It grows all year round in the woods or near water. It loses its stinging properties when boiled in water and becomes quite delicious.

Sparrowgrass or wild asparagus (*Asparagus officinalis*) is an upright white or green shoot that emerges from the ground to form a bushy plant. It usually grows near deciduous woods in spring.

Look in your botany or foraging guide for the herbs that grow in city parks or in the natural areas you plan to explore, cataloguing as many in your herbarium as possible.

Use your journal to catalogue the wild herbs you find as you are walking. Remember that not all spontaneous plants are entirely edible. In some cases only one part can be eaten, in others you need to wait until the plant reaches a specific phase of growth before you can eat it. You should always check your botany manual or other reliable sources, and you must absolutely avoid eating any plants you cannot positively identify.

Trees You Can Eat

Nothing puts us more in contact with our natural side than eating directly from a tree. I do not mean you should climb a tree and eat its leaves like a koala, but try to consider broad-leaved and fir trees as an incredible source of food.

Some trees have edible parts that can be extracted or picked and eaten, often without being cooked. Consult a botany or foraging manual to discover which of the species in your area offer the most edible parts.

You will see how many species have edible bark, leaves, twigs, seeds, pollens, roots, sprouts, flowers, and sap. For example, you can eat the inner bark of the birch tree (*Betula*), known as phloem, and the tree's young leaves can be cooked as a leafy vegetable in spring. The birch tree is also full of sap that we can tap and drink. The sap extracted from the European white birch (*Betula verrucosa*) has been used for centuries for the many well-known health benefits it brings to the human body. As a natural remedy, it has remarkable detoxifying, diuretic, anti-inflammatory, and analgesic applications.

Extend your search to include the edible parts of trees such as beech, basswood, maple, mulberry, walnut, aspen, oak, willow, and many conifers, such as the Norway spruce.

Use your journal to catalogue the trees that offer edible parts that you find along your walk. Draw the tree and, as you do, try to reproduce the parts that most characterize it, such as its leaves, bark, seeds, fruit, and flowers. Always research each species thoroughly. Learn as much as you can about it and the ways its edible parts can be used in cooking. Always check a botany manual or some other reliable sources, and never eat something you cannot positively identify.

The Fungus Population

Alongside the animal, plant, and mineral kingdoms, there is the vast realm of fungi, made of millions of species distributed all over the world. Fungi are neither plants nor animals, but something completely different, almost a hybrid between the two categories. These curious living beings are made of long thin filaments called *hyphae*, formed by very long cells located underground, where they form a network, called *mycelium*. What we commonly see sprouting is just the "fruit."

Like animals—and unlike plants—fungi do not know how to produce the nutrients they need to live, and they can survive without light. To reproduce, they entrust their spores to the wind or to animals. They have no elements that carry sap, and they feed on organic substances synthesized from other organisms. They take the nutrients they need in three ways:

Saprophytic fungi chemically alter and absorb substances from plants or animal carcasses; parasitic fungi get nutrients from living organisms, potentially killing them; and finally, symbiotic fungi live in symbiosis with their host plant with reciprocal benefits. They feed on their host without harming it, as we have seen in the underground network of hyphae that connect trees and exchange nutrients with the roots they colonize.

When you find a mushroom, examine it closely. Take a picture of it, or sketch it in your journal so you can discover more about it later, either from a mycology manual or from a mycologist. If it is edible, catalogue it in your herbarium with an accurate description. Never eat a mushroom unless you are absolutely sure that it is edible.

When you see a mushroom you would like to pick, cut it at its base with your pocketknife, leaving behind the filaments that connect it to the ground. Do not destroy the inedible mushrooms you find; they are useful for the environment. Use your foraging tools to pick and transport the ones you want; and when you have no doubt whatsoever about their edibility, draw them on a page in your journal to add them to your herbarium. Once again, be sure to consult a botany manual or some other reliable source, and never eat something you are unable to positively identify.

Hunting for Lichens

In 1867, the botanist Simon Schwender defined lichen as an organism formed by the symbiosis between a fungus and an algae. The algae uses photosynthesis to produce nutrients for the fungus, which furnishes the water and mineral salts necessary for the algae to survive. Lichens grow very slowly and, in fact, they progress just a few millimeters a year, but they can live for centuries in the most adverse conditions.

You can gather and eat many species of lichens, but you must be careful; these organisms absorb the toxic substances present in the air, so gather them only in uncontaminated areas.

Many lichens grow on trees, covering their trunks with a sage green color. One of these is oakmoss (*Evernia prunastri*), which in addition to being edible is used as a wood-scented fragrance. The reindeer lichen (*Cladonia rangiferina*) grows in the Arctic tundra, where reindeer and caribou feast on it. The manna lichen (*Lecanora esculenta*) grows in the desert, where the sun dries it and the wind lifts it into the air, from where it drops back to earth like snow. It was the famous manna that the Jews ate during their biblical exile. Rock tripe (*Umbilicaria esculenta*), also known as rock ear, is widespread in eastern Asia and is commonly eaten in Japan, Korea, and China. *Girophora umbilicaria* is also known as rock tripe, and it is said that George Washington and his troops survived on it during the famine of 1777.

The treatment that lichens have to undergo to make them edible is a long process. Eaten raw, they have an acidic flavor and a consistency that makes them unsuitable for consumption. They may contain toxic substances as well.

Compare the shapes and colors of the lichens you find with those in a botany guide to see if the ones you have found are edible. If you find Iceland moss (*Cetraria islandica*), you can use it as a calming liquid for your skin, or you can use it to make a decoction.

ICELAND MOSS DECOCTION

You can prepare a decoction with Iceland moss to take internally for bronchial inflammation. Use 1/2 teaspoon (2 g) of dried thallus (the vegetative tissue of the lichen) in 0.4 cups (100 ml) of water. To mitigate the bitter taste of the lichen, you can first boil it briefly, then drain the water and add more water to make the final decoction. Drink two or three cups a day.

The same decoction can be used externally to wash with, dabbing it on your skin with cotton wherever necessary.

Let a handful of Iceland moss steep in your bath water to purify and soften your skin.

Culturing Our Bacterial Microcosm

Fermentation is a process that transforms foods with active bacteria to make them more digestible and nourishing. Since the process is very ancient, recipes to ferment food exist in every corner of the world, in every culinary tradition. Even in our culture, we put a number of food products on the table that have undergone fermentation: for example, beer, wine and other beverages, cheese, miso, yogurt, and many more.

At one time, this technique was used primarily to conserve food. The microorganisms that activate the fermentation process produce alcohol, lactic acid, and acetic acid, all of which are organic preservatives that keep nutrients intact and prevent the formation of pathogenic bacteria. Reclaiming the artisanal use of fermentation at home means taming useful bacteria and rediscovering how nature can help us make food more healthful and more interesting from a culinary point of view.

Besides modifying the look and the taste of foods, fermentation also makes them easier to preserve and digest. In addition, it triggers the formation of acids that lower the food's pH and inhibit the development of harmful microorganisms, thereby making the food more resistant to colonization by pathogenic bacteria. The vitamin content of foods also increases during the fermentation process, making the food more healthful and more nourishing. The most widespread forms of fermentation are those using alcohol, lactic acid, and acetic acid.

To culture bacteria that will make your food more healthful and tastier is a wonderful way to study the infinite possibilities nature can bring to our diet if we understand how it works.

To begin to experiment with fermentation, get yourself a *scoby*, a cellulose mat that holds bacteria and yeast cultures used to make *kombucha*, a tart and slightly sweet fermented tea. This tea, which is simple to prepare, has many beneficial properties, including strengthening your immune system.

KOMBUCHA

Ingredients and equipment

- 3.8 cups (900 ml) mineral water (avoid water with chlorine)
- 0.5 oz (15 g) black tea
- 3.5 oz (100 g) sugar
- 0.4 cups (100 ml) of prepared *kombucha* (if you are preparing it for the first time, increase the water to 4.2 cups/1 l)
- 1 *scoby* (you can buy it or get it from someone who already has one)
- 1 large wide-mouth jar
- 1 paper napkin or paper towel to cover the jar and a rubber band to keep it in place

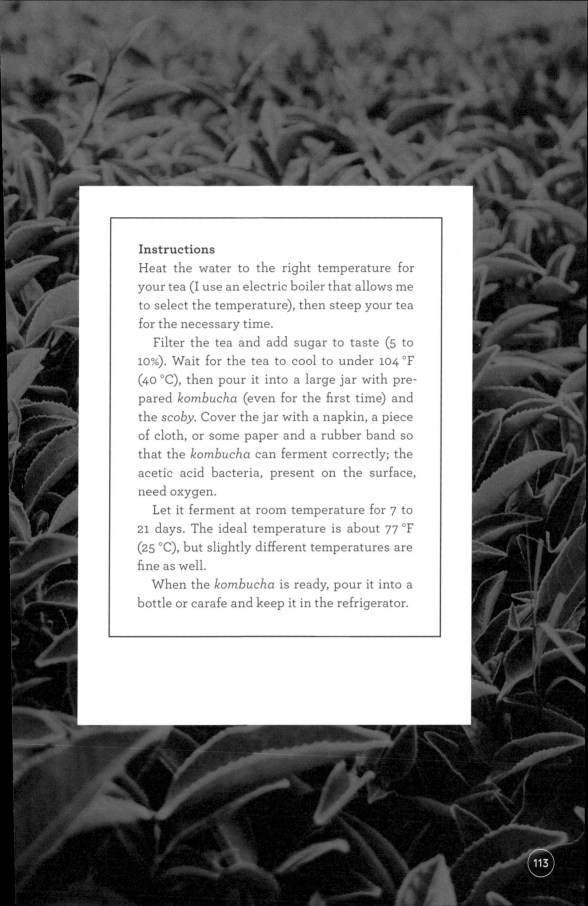

Instructions

Heat the water to the right temperature for your tea (I use an electric boiler that allows me to select the temperature), then steep your tea for the necessary time.

Filter the tea and add sugar to taste (5 to 10%). Wait for the tea to cool to under 104 °F (40 °C), then pour it into a large jar with prepared *kombucha* (even for the first time) and the *scoby*. Cover the jar with a napkin, a piece of cloth, or some paper and a rubber band so that the *kombucha* can ferment correctly; the acetic acid bacteria, present on the surface, need oxygen.

Let it ferment at room temperature for 7 to 21 days. The ideal temperature is about 77 °F (25 °C), but slightly different temperatures are fine as well.

When the *kombucha* is ready, pour it into a bottle or carafe and keep it in the refrigerator.

A Chef in Nature

The time has come to use what we have gathered in our foraging expeditions to make a dish. Adding what we have foraged to what we cook is a fundamental way to get to know nature better and connect to it.

I suggest you look through cookbooks to find either modern or ancient recipes that include wild ingredients you pick yourself.

The many chefs present on social media who have contributed heavily to the rediscovery of wild ingredients in cuisine can surely give you a tip or two. There is an entire group of chefs who dabble in wild ingredients, including René Redzepi from the Noma restaurant in Copenhagen, who surprises us every day with new reflections about the use of foraging in cuisine; Alex Atala from the D.O.M. Restaurant in Brazil, who forages ingredients in the Amazon jungle; Heinz Reitbauer from the Steirereck restaurant in Vienna, who delights diners with dishes like nasturtium with chufa, elderberry flowers, and clover; Norbert Niederkofler in the South Tyrol, who focuses on the natural resources of the Dolomites; and Valeria Margherita Mosca from the Wooding Lab in Italy, who teaches us how to make dishes, both elaborate and simple, with extraordinary flavor using wild ingredients.

Make a note in your journal of all the modern or traditional recipes you find that use wild ingredients. To prepare your dishes, you can take ideas from existing recipes, or create something completely new, playing with flavor combinations and contrasts, and with the textures of the ingredients you have foraged. Just be completely sure that what you are using is edible and harmless to your health.

RISOTTO WITH WILD HERBS AND PRIMO SALE CHEESE

Ingredients (for four servings)

- 8.8 oz (250 g) of Carnaroli rice
- 1 bunch of wild herbs
  (I recommend ribwort and nettles)
- 1 spring onion
- 7 oz (200 g) of Primo Sale cheese
- 3 tbsp of grated Parmigiano Reggiano
- 3 cups (700 ml) of vegetable broth
- 2 tbsp of extra virgin olive oil
- 2 tbsp of fresh thyme leaves
- Salt and pepper to taste

Instructions

Wash the wild herbs you have foraged under running water and blot them on a paper towel to dry, and then chop them into small pieces. Peel and chop the spring onion, cut the Primo Sale cheese into small bits, and heat the broth.

In a large saucepan, sauté the onion with a tablespoon of extra virgin olive oil, then add the chopped herbs and let them develop their flavor over a low flame for two or three minutes and adjust the seasoning. Add the rice to the saucepan and let it toast for two minutes.

Add one ladle of broth at a time, tasting often to check the consistency, until the rice is cooked. The risotto should be dense and creamy. Adjust salt and pepper, and mix in the primo sale cheese, the Parmigiano, and the remaining olive oil. Season your risotto with thyme, then mix and serve.

Chapter 4

IN THE WILD

The Native American Lesson

....

"My friend, I am going to tell you the story of my life, as you wish; and if it were only the story of my life, I think I would not tell it; for what is one man that he should make much of his winters, even when they bend him like a heavy snow? So many other men have lived and shall live that story, to be grass upon the hills. It is the story of all life that is holy and is good to tell, and of us two-leggeds sharing in it with the four-leggeds and the wings of the air and all green things; for these are children of one mother, and their father is one Spirit."

This is the lesson that Black Elk, the spiritual guide of the Ogla-la tribe, gave to the American historian and ethnographer John G. Neihardt in a famous interview. In 1932, the entire conversation was written and published in the book *Black Elk Speaks*, which was extremely successful throughout the world. The Oglala Lakota are one of the seven bands of the southern Lakota or Teton Sioux tribes whose descendants still live on reservations in the United States.

Today, the entire conversation between Black Elk and Neihardt is an interesting testimonial to the lives of some Native Americans groups, their social organizations, and the spiritual foundations that influence their cultures and traditions.

The infamous massacre at Wounded Knee took place at the end of December 1890 and is generally considered the end of the "Indian Wars" or conflicts between colonial forces and native people. The Miniconjou tribe, led by Big Foot, heard of the murder of Sitting Bull and left their camp at Cherry Creek to go to Pine Ridge, hoping that Red Cloud, the chief of the Teton Oglala tribe, would protect them. On December 28, four cavalry squadrons of the Seventh Regiment, led by Major Samuel Whitside, intercepted 120 men and 230 women and children and massacred them. Black Elk was seriously wounded but survived, and he was able to tell the story of the battle to a writer.

The colonizers came bearing their self-styled "superior civilization" and perpetrated environmental devastation and murder that decimated entire communities that had lived in the area for thousands of years. The tribes present in the US today may be geographically distant from one another in terms of customs and traditions, but many Native groups feel a close bond with their environment and its lands, animals, and plants. Some Native American traditions consider animals, rocks, and trees part of the same great family as beings conceived by the mind of the Great Spirit, the supreme being and creator of every existing thing, the giver of life to forests, meadows, streams, and the Sun, away from which humans could never stray or they would be condemned to suffering and destruction.

Looking at the environmental emergencies that have recently neared the point of no return, we must accept that protecting nature is an act of safeguarding our communities and ourselves. We must find the way to a future where plants, animals, and humans live in harmony and balance.

Our journey continues with other practices that can help us find a path to peacefully share our planet with animals and plantlife. Books like *Braiding Sweetgrass* are a great place to start.

Being Nature

In a system that partially overrides the IQ index for evaluating human intelligence, the American psychologist Howard Gardner proposed eight types of intelligence that are present in each of us in varying degrees. One of these is so-called naturalistic intelligence, the eighth manifestation of human intelligence, according to the classification in his "theory of multiple intelligences." It is defined as the ability to enter into a profound connection with nonhuman living beings and improve the effect that this relationship has on us and on the environment.

Giuseppe Barbiero, professor of Biology and Ecopsychology and director of the Laboratory of Affective Ecology at the University of Valle d'Aosta, defines "biophilia" as our love for living nature. This definition of biophilia holds that all living things attract us and create emotions that can lead to a sincere bond with nature when correctly guided. Biophilia is an innate predisposition, but it is not instinctive, and therefore it must be stimulated if we want it to develop. One way to stimulate it is to seek contact with our inner selves and the environment in which we live—for example, through mindfulness meditation. So, if nature and the wilderness can regenerate the human psyche, the human psyche in turn can use the awareness (mindfulness) of emotions to establish a strong connection to the planet. This would have important implications for environmental protection, respect for the ecosystems, the study of nature, and general well-being.

Therefore, practicing meditation and exploring the beautiful practice of mindfulness will be very helpful to our re-wilding process.

MINDFULNESS

The mindfulness or awareness that we are speaking of here refers to our ability to pay attention to our desires, our emotions, and the present moment in an objective, detached way, free from any judgment. Dedicating a few minutes each day to this practice has a number of benefits, including more open-mindedness, a profound sense of well-being, and a feeling of connection with the universe.

To practice mindful meditation, lie down on a mat or get comfortable in a chair, with your eyes open and your back straight. Focus on your breathing and become aware of it.

There are many ways to do this. I suggest focusing on the coolness and warmth of the air as it passes through your nostrils each time you inhale and exhale. Initially, ten minutes divided into two five-minute sessions a day is enough, and as the days go by, it will become easier and easier to free your mind of thoughts.

Once you become more comfortable with your meditation, you can increase the time of each session. Practice will increase your resistance, as it does with any activity. Constant, regular meditation will make you better at it; your awareness can be extended from your breath to your thoughts and then to your feelings and actions. At that point, your level of connection to your environment and your inner self will have increased enormously.

Invent a Fairy Tale Set in Nature

A fairy tale or fable—from the word *fabula* in Latin, meaning a story or narration—is a story told in verse or in prose in which the characters are often animals who can think and talk, or, more rarely, are humans or objects. Its purpose is to teach something by example or to demonstrate a moral.

An exercise that can be useful in your journey to reconnection is to use the language of fables to create and tell a story that has a significant moral for you. For example, you can express the sacredness of friendship, of unity among people, of the respect for animals and plants, or any other thing that is deeply important to you.

Use the memories of your excursions into nature to create a setting for your fairy tale. This will give you a chance to recall the images of nature that you have assimilated during the course of your re-wilding. Remembering the places you discovered and with which you formed a particular bond—a path, a forest, a tree, a rock, or a meadow—gives you the opportunity to bring life to the images and feelings you experienced in nature and create a very deep connection with it. As the main characters of your fairy tale, choose one or more animals that could actually live in the setting you have chosen, so you can convey to your listener some of the knowledge you have acquired during your explorations. In the mountains, your characters could be deer or marmots; it will be easy to give shape to their personalities. As you develop your story, tell it to someone who will give you feedback to help refine the structure and make it linear and enjoyable, for both the teller and the listener.

When you think your fairy tale is ready, write it down in a journal and give it a title. Then use that journal to collect all the stories you create; they will become a precious memory that you can recall and share in the future. You can also illustrate your fairy tale with the images in your mind.

TWO LITTLE BROTHERS IN A TREE

This is the story of two little squirrels who lived happily in the trunk and branches of the tallest larch in the forest. The air was beginning to get cool, and they knew that the long winter was coming and that they would have to survive it without going into hibernation.

The two were very different; one was strong and brave, and the other was more frail and pensive. One night, they were awakened by a wolf who was circling their tree trunk and staring up at them. He was famished, and he looked like he was determined to wait for the right moment to capture a snack. The squirrels decided it was best not to climb down from the tree, and they spent a number of days there, hoping in vain that the wolf would grow tired of waiting.

When they realized that they would not be able to leave the tree before the beginning of winter, they gathered all the food they had: just one acorn and a small hazelnut. The smaller squirrel accidentally dropped the hazelnut on the wolf, who looked up at the two, licking his lips. The stronger squirrel was afraid and wanted to keep the remaining acorn all for himself. In refusing to share it with his brother, he betrayed the tacit pact of mutual aid they had always respected. The smaller squirrel ran away, up the tree trunk, crying desperately. He climbed and climbed until he reached the highest branches, where he had never been before.

There, he discovered a hole in the trunk that led to an abandoned stash of acorns and other woodland delicacies. The first thing he did was to run and tell his brother what he had found, and that they were finally safe and had enough food for the entire winter!

His brother understood the serious betrayal he had committed and filled with shame begged for forgiveness; and after a great feast, the two fell asleep in the coziness of a brotherly embrace.

Lighting a Small Campfire

Primitive humans discovered the use of fire during the Lower Paleolithic period, an era that lasted from about 2.5 million to 120,000 years ago. In that period, they began to tame the spontaneous fires caused by lightning and other natural events in order to warm themselves; cook meat, making it more tender and digestible; and find comfort during long prehistoric nights. Around the campfires of thousands of years ago, social ties were formed and dissolved, stories were told that were then handed down for thousands of years, knowledge and information were exchanged, and rituals and banquets that brought the community together were celebrated. The time has come for us to rediscover this ancient practice as well, and to experience the same sensations our ancestors did as they looked for comfort in nature's wilderness.

Before lighting a campfire, carefully choose a suitable place and check that conditions are favorable. Prepare the area you have chosen, clearing away anything that could be flammable; and then, if possible, surround the area with stones big enough to contain your fire. In the middle of the circle of stones, prepare a cushion of kindling with dry pine needles, lichens, and small dry twigs. Cover the kindling partially with a pile of small dry branches that will light easily, and then lay at least three thicker pieces of firewood around them, along with any other wood that you have gathered. To light the kindling, you will need a flint or firestone (you can buy one in shops that sell outdoor equipment), or you can create a spark by striking the blade of a knife on a stone. The sparks that fall on the kindling will begin to produce smoke and small flames that will get bigger and bigger until the campfire is completely burning. If you prefer to simplify your life, you can always use matches or a lighter.

Make a note in your journal of the materials you used for kindling and how you arranged the rest of the wood. Make a sketch of your fire to help you remember where you put the bigger pieces of wood and whether or not it was functional. When you light your first campfire, sit down close to it in a position where the smoke will not reach you. Write down the feelings you have, the noises you hear, and the colors you see. Make sure to observe the rules of safety and, if you can, make your first campfire with someone who has more experience than you do.

FIRE AND SAFETY

To light a campfire that is safe for ourselves and for the surrounding environment, there are some rules that must be closely followed and some suitable behaviors to adopt. Here are the golden rules for safely lighting a fire in the wilderness:

- check with local authorities that lighting fires in the area is not prohibited;
- don't light fires under overhanging branches or along steep slopes;
- always have water or a spade on hand to extinguish an out-of-control fire;
- always keep the size of a campfire contained or proportionate to the number of people around it;
- never leave a campfire unattended;
- after extinguishing the flame, cover the campfire with plenty of water and soil, stirring repeatedly and adding more water to make sure there are no more small burning embers;
- never simply bury burning coals. They can continue to burn under the soil and ignite roots, causing uncontrolled fires;
- avoid lighting a campfire on a windy day.

Visiting Our Totem Tree

The relationship between trees and humans is deep and ancient. There is much sacred symbology involving trees: consider the totems of many ancient peoples, sacred staffs used by shamans and priests, and the columns of the classical temples, which not only symbolize the heavens but also the solid roots in the depths of the earth.

Choosing a tree and making it the object of our personal tribute, and visiting it frequently, is a practice that can reinforce our reconnection with nature.

When we choose our tree, we establish a relationship full of stimuli that will lead us to reflect and contemplate the value of plants, of the land, and of the creatures that live there. Enjoying the shade under your tree in the summer, watching as its colors change, noting small differences as the seasons pass, studying the slow process of growth and healing, noticing the animals that visit it or use it for nesting and breeding, all mean entering into a relationship of empathy with another living being and witnessing its existence. Even thinking about our tree from time to time when we are far from it lets us establish contact with the natural territory where it lives and reawaken the emotions we feel when we visit.

We might choose our tree by chance, when we are attracted by a plant that we feel a particular empathy for during a walk, but we can also search for our chosen tree, once we have decided to strike up a privileged relationship with a plant creature. In that case, we will choose a tree that attracts us with its shape, fragrance, flowers, or fruit.

A relationship with a tree is built similarly to the way you build one with a person: with your presence, constancy, attention, and the willingness to meet. When you choose or find your tree, write the dates you visit it in your journal, and draw or describe your plant and the changes you notice from time to time.

Visiting the Forest at Night

The forest has always held a strong fascination for humans, to the point that they have set hundreds of fairy tales, myths, and legends full of esoteric aspects, mystery, and evil presences there. After all, the fairy tales of the Brothers Grimm would be much less intriguing without the dense forest where Hansel and Gretel run into an evil witch who tries to devour them as they wander, in search of their way home. And how different would Little Red Riding Hood's story be if she could have reached her grandmother's house without going through the forest, where she met a ferocious wolf who would swallow her in one bite? In each of these stories, the forest is a place of terror where evil hides.

There is even a clinical term, *nyctohylophobia,* to describe the fear of the forest at night. The word comes from the union of the Greek words *hylophobia*, the irrational fear of wooded areas, and *nyctophobia*, the fear of the dark. Psychologists explain that a walk in the forest at night could be unsettling for many of us, because it evokes fearsome myths and popular beliefs, which can be overcome or debunked with experience and knowledge. At this point, our re-wilding journey has taught us to understand the dynamics of nature and the natural environment. We now realize that a forest is just as safe at night as it is during the day, with the only difference being that it will probably be colder and will be populated by nocturnal animals, some of whom may have earned themselves an unfair reputation as witch-like or malignant creatures. The owl and the wolf, for example, are both creatures that are often associated with witchcraft, mystery, or death. Some also fear that the woods may be home to ill-intentioned or dangerous people, without realizing that if this were a real concern, walking in the city would be much more dangerous.

Find a wooded area not too far from home to begin your nocturnal explorations. Always be sure to tell someone about your plans and dress in such a way as to stay dry and warm for the whole walk. Take a flashlight or a headlamp; it will help you avoid getting lost. Observe the environment around you and think about what you feel in nature in the dark. Remember that fear of the forest at night is normal, but the fear should be free of biased beliefs and superstitions.

Presence

How nice would it be to smell the scent of fir trees, to hear the singing of birds, and to feel the coolness of the mountain air when we are stuck in traffic?

Well, there is a very effective way to become part of the environment we are visiting and call it to mind later. It involves doing something for nature with our hands and minds, rather than interacting as mere spectators or beneficiaries of its wonders.

It is easier to evoke the memory of the natural places we visit if we leave a part of ourselves there. Doing so serves as a kind of umbilical cord, establishing a deep, lasting bond that allows the boundaries of our home, our safe place, to expand beyond the domestic walls and conquer spaces that will become familiar. It is important that nothing we do in the natural place where we seek connections distort the place itself, and that nothing remain there for long. For example, when we are on a walk, we can make what are known as rock cairns, man-made piles of rocks that resemble small totem poles. They indicate the way when path signs or tracks are imprecise or absent. Or we can build a small hut to use as a bivouac, or decorate branches or the ground with natural materials we find around us.

As you walk, choose materials that attract your attention, observe them, make a composition that you like with them, and then leave it there and go on your way.

LAND ART

Exploring the bond between your brain and your environment, and reflecting on your reconnection to nature through your actions, is one of the pillars of Land Art, a modern art form born in the late 1960s in the US. The artist intervenes directly in a natural territory that may be an unspoiled space in the desert, a lake, a meadow, or a forest.

I admire the work of the artist and photographer Andy Goldsworthy, who is also a pioneer of rock balancing, the art of piling stones in perfect balance to create truly amazing sculptures. His works make us reflect on the fragility and mutability of nature, and on the perpetuation of the present moment, in which the artist modifies the history or the shape of the natural place he visits, even if only for a moment, and forms a deep empathic bond with it. Photography is the tool used to fix the work of art—which will disappear in a matter of days—in our memory.

With Your Nose in the Air at Night

Observing a star-filled sky at night is an exciting experience for all of us, from the time we are children. The desire to be up there with the stars and imagining traveling into space to see the planets, the constellations, and the universe up close makes children want to become astronauts one day. The word "desire" comes from the Latin word *sidera,* meaning stars, preceded by the prefix *de-*, meaning missing, so we could translate the word "desire" to mean "missing the stars," or needing the stars, just as the seafarers did to map their routes.

Getting to know the sky, and understanding how the cosmos and the rules that govern it work, make us aware that we are part of a boundless complex mechanism. When we look at the night sky, it is natural for us to ponder our role as living beings in relation to the infinity of space and time. Above all else, we become aware that our planet is a giant spaceship, suspended in the void of space.

The first thing astronauts do when they arrive in orbit is to look down and admire the Earth. All of them say they were overwhelmed by the "overview effect," the sudden cognitive change caused by observing Earth from space for the first time. Mind, emotions, spirituality, and environmental consciousness are overwhelmed by the dramatic shift in perspective that occurs during space travel, when our planet suddenly appears as a fragile sphere in the enormity of the universe, as a unique place that we must learn to preserve.

When we go out into nature at the end of the day and the sky turns dark, we have a chance to enjoy the spectacle of a celestial dome sparkling with stars. We can look for the various constellations and memorize their positions; observe the moon and identify its phase at that moment; and find the visible planets and their positions at that specific time of the year, using a map of the sky.

There are apps we can use to identify celestial bodies, using augmented reality. If we look closely, even with the naked eye, we can see some of the many artificial satellites that circle our planet—and perhaps even the International Space Station, where people like us are working and maybe peering down from time to time to admire our planet from up there.

If you are out in nature on a clear night, you can observe the stars, the moon, the planets, and the constellations. Try to recognize the celestial bodies you see, use your journal to make note of them, and draw their positions in the sky at a specific moment of the year. Use a compass to locate a useful reference point for your observation. When you are finished, memorize the names of the lunar phases and constellations you have observed, as well as anything else that caught your attention.

THE MOON AND THE LUNAR PHASES

The moon, our planet's only natural satellite, orbits at approximately 238,855 miles (384,400 km) from earth.

The moon is gravitationally (or "tidally") locked in synchronous rotation with the earth; "synchronous" means that the orbiting body always shows the same face to the body around which it orbits, so the moon always shows the same face to the earth, regardless of the point of observation on the earth. The various lunar phases depend on the moon's position as it orbits the earth—and with respect to the sun.

Seen from the earth, the moon is sometimes completely illuminated, sometimes only partially illuminated, and sometimes completely dark. These lunar phases are repeated in the same order every month, in what is called a synodic or lunar cycle that lasts 29 days, 12 hours, and 44 minutes. The four main lunar phases are the new moon, first quarter, full moon, and last quarter. The intermediate phases, beginning after the new moon, between these are respectively the waxing (or rising) moon, waxing (or rising) gibbous, waning gibbous, and waning moon. Although there is no scientific evidence, the waxing moon is thought to favor the development of plants, since it is the time that sap tends to come toward the surface. Conversely, with the waning moon, sap retreats toward the roots, so many believe that the waning moon is propitious for planting.

Our Home Is Everywhere

As children, we often wished for a small secret shelter in nature, where we could go for a snack with our friends and feel like we were adventurers in the middle of the wilderness, protected by a safe place we'd built with our own hands.

We can do that as adults as well because, regardless of our age, building a shelter or protected space in nature has many important effects. First of all, using our hands to realize a small project that we have imagined increases our creativity and stimulates our problem-solving skills. Finding the right materials and using them to build our structure is not easy—it requires focus and dedication—but, in the end, seeing what we have made with our own hands will be exciting, and we will remember the feeling for a long time. Going into our hut in the middle of nature will make us feel completely protected, even in a space that is far from home, teaching us that our concept of being shielded and protected can and should be extended beyond the walls of our homes.

We can build our first hut by simply leaning or tying two long sticks of similar length that are solid, not old or rotting, to the trunk of a tree, one next to the other at a 45° angle. We will need to fill the space between the sticks with smaller ones to complete the structure, and then cover it with leaves and twigs. We can leave a portion of one side uncovered to make an entryway. Let's go into our hut and enjoy the excitement of feeling at home.

> Look for suitable materials in the area you are exploring, and build your own little hut; then take a picture of it or draw it. Try to memorize its location and note it in your journal, but leave the hut standing when you leave; it will be a nice surprise when you go back there, or it can be used as shelter from the rain or cold for other explorers like yourself.

Barefoot

Researchers from the University of California, Irvine first published the results of a study they conducted in the journal *Environmental and Public Health* in 2012. They illustrated the positive effects on the body and mind of a practice called grounding, or walking barefoot in nature to reclaim natural spaces and reap the benefits of direct bodily contact with the land. The practice is well known in yoga and other Oriental disciplines such as *t'ai chi ch'uan* and *qi gong.*

In past centuries, when humans lived most of their lives barefoot, having contact with the earth made the soles of their feet strong and resistant and gave them a more natural posture.

We can still experience that contact today by removing our shoes and walking for hours on the beach, on stones, in the grass, or in the woods. We will enjoy a profound sense of freedom and an extraordinary feeling of reconnection to the land we are walking through. The muscles in the arches of our feet, our ankles, and our shins accumulate a surprising amount of energy; and during the day, our bodies are charged with positive electrons. These come into contact with the negative particles in the ground when we walk barefoot, and our electrostatic charge is rebalanced, which brings great benefits to our stress level, immune system, mood, and much more.

Granting ourselves a moment with no shoes gives us the opportunity to form a more authentic relationship with the environment that surrounds us, by compelling us to walk more slowly and to carefully choose where we put our feet. It is an opportunity to choose our own personal pathway and to become more aware of our uniqueness as individuals.

When you are out in nature, take off your shoes and socks and put them in your backpack. With your bare feet, try to feel the temperature of the earth, the roughness of the stones, the softness of the moss and grass, and the coolness of the water you walk through. Focus on the sensations you get from this part of your walk. Try to prolong this grounding session for as long as you can; the results will be surprising.

Dreaming Under the Stars

Sleeping under the stars, far from home and surrounded by nature, is one of the most meaningful, exciting experiences for those who are seeking to truly reconnect with nature. Spending our first night under the stars, lying in the grass or in comfortable bedding, does not require a lot of equipment or preparation. All we need are a bit of outfitting, some courage, and our spirit of adventure.

Sleeping in the open can be a tactical choice for hikers who want to stay out more than one day without carrying a tent and other heavy equipment; but for some it is a choice dictated by the pure pleasure of falling asleep under the immense starry sky, with its magic and charm.

Carefully check weather forecasts to avoid rain and storms when you plan to sleep in the open. Choose a mild season and bring equipment that will keep you warm and dry, including a sleeping bag suitable to the weather (consider the predicted wind-chill effect, as well as the temperature), a mat that insulates you from the moisture that the ground releases at night, and a plastic sheet to cover yourself with so the moisture cannot settle on the top of your sleeping bag. Bring a cotton or wool cap to wear under the hood of your sleeping bag, and do not forget to bring a flashlight or headlamp. It will be useful as you prepare your bed and stow your things in your backpack, which you can use as a pillow. Before you get into your sleeping bag, take off your shoes and, if the weather permits, your clothes too.

Prepare for the excursion that will include your first night sleeping in the open. If you decide to go alone, always tell someone about your plans. Listen carefully to the emotions this experience triggers in you, and remember that feeling afraid is completely normal. The thought of falling asleep and being attacked by animals or people is part of a legacy we can eliminate only through experience. Watching the sun rise after sleeping in the open will make you feel stronger, and it will increase your confidence and your sense of connection to nature.

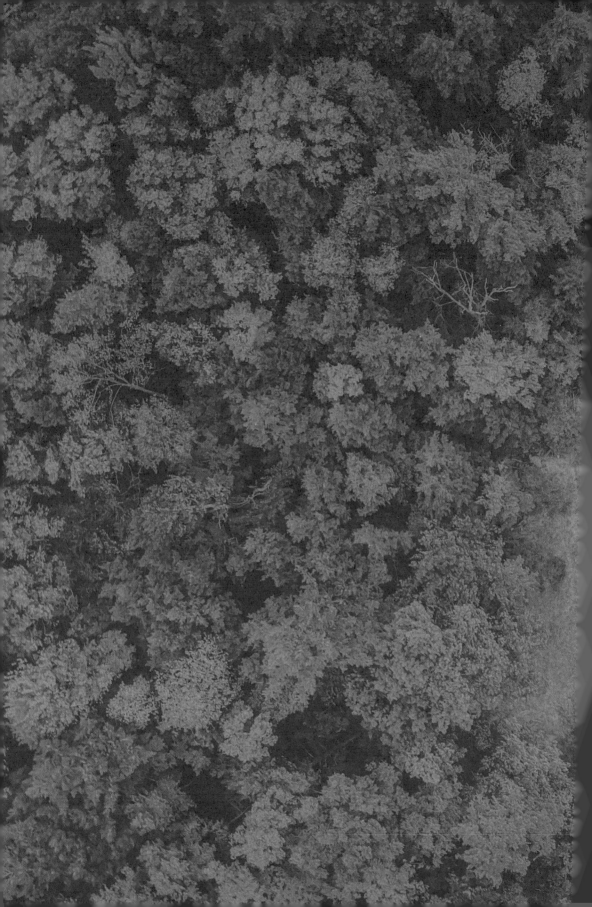

Chapter 5

EXPERIENCING NATURE

Sustainability and Indicators of Well-being

····················

When we consider a natural habitat, we have to ask ourselves if the exploitation of its resources for human activities is sustainable in the long run. In brief, this is what we define as "environmental sustainability," a commonly used term in a variety of areas today, ranging from scientific conferences on climate change to marketing campaigns for products and services.

It is impossible to deny that, until now, we have produced, distributed, and consumed all kinds of goods without really considering what they "cost" in terms of deforestation, soil quality and quantity, air quality, and the availability of water and other resources necessary for the survival of plants, animals, and human beings. We have reached a critical point at which we are using more natural resources than the planet can regenerate. Earth Overshoot Day is the day when humans have exhausted the resources that the earth is able to regenerate for the current year. It is a disturbing fact that this day arrives earlier and earlier each year.

By the middle of the year, most industrialized countries have already exhausted their renewable natural resources, which means that to reach the end of the year and meet industrial production and consumption goals, they would need the resources equivalent to or exceeding those available on two "Planet Earths." It is clearly urgent that we create new economic and production models that have a lower impact on our natural resources, to avoid the impoverishment of biodiversity and the worsening of the quality of life for all of us.

In fact, recent studies highlight the impact of pollution, climate change, and other side effects of industrialization on the collective happiness of nations and their citizens.

Bhutan, a small Buddhist kingdom located in the Asian Himalayan area, is proposing an interesting scientific index that measures the collective well-being of its citizens. It takes into account both the wealth produced by the economy and the level of happiness of the country's inhabitants. This index has been called the GNH, or "gross national happiness," as purposely opposed to the GDP, the gross domestic product, which measures the value of products and services a nation produces and sells in a given period of time. GDP is clearly limited as the definition of a nation's well-being. Such a definition must include the loss of irreplaceable natural wealth, such as glaciers, animal species, forests, and any other resources that are exploited to produce riches, and the impact that this loss has on the happiness and future living conditions of its citizens.

Factors such as air quality, the health of ecosystems, the health and education of citizens, and the richness of social relationships are taken into account to calculate GNH. Other similar "well-being metrics" are useful for assessing the impact that environmental issues have on happiness.

In fact, the lifestyles and the logic associated with the current global economy create air pollution and the effects of climate change, and they generate costs. These costs can be measured in terms of the dissatisfaction of people living with these effects when compared to the people who live in greener urban or coastal areas and are reportedly happier.

Bhutan's goal is to guarantee that the happiness of its citizens be the only purpose of economic development.

The GNH index has undergone some changes over the years, becoming a more quantitative indicator, in part because of the unexpected global interest it has sparked. Today, it can be defined as a multidimensional approach to development that aims to reach an equilibrium between material well-being and the spiritual, emotional, and cultural needs of society.

The key word here is "balance," which can be accomplished by creating an equilibrium between the needs of the body and the mind, and between the needs of the economy and nature. This index has not been officially adopted by the planet's industrialized countries, but the discordant relationship between wealth and happiness has become very evident to many. Nature and the feeling of connection to it play a key role in this relationship and heavily influence the level of individual happiness.

Completing a journey of re-wilding and reconnection to nature appears to be a responsibility we should accept for the collective good.

It is fundamental for every nation to favor relationships with nature, thought quality, physical well-being, spirituality, and the quality of the social relationships of its citizens as much as it favors economic solidity and prosperity.

Waking Up

In 1937, after the success of his movie *Lost Horizon*, which gained Frank Capra recognition as a notable director in Hollywood, a young writer by the name of Peter Kelder rolled up his sleeves and began writing the screenplay for another movie that he imagined in Tibet, in the Himalayans. It told the story of the elderly Colonel Bradford, an official in the British Army who learned the secret of eternal youth from some Tibetan monks and returned to his homeland, surprisingly rejuvenated.

In 1949, the screenplay was adapted and became one of the first personal growth guides in history, called *The Five Tibetans*. Kelder's book, *The Ancient Secret of the Fountain of Youth*, reveals that the secret of living a long and healthy life is to perform simple daily movements that resemble *asana* or yoga poses, and that everyone or almost everyone can do. When the book was rediscovered and republished in the 1980s, it became a global success because the exercises proposed by Kelder seemed to bring truly extraordinary benefits to the mind and body.

Today many people can testify to the fact that routinely performing the five Tibetan rites greatly increases vital energy and improves skin, hair, the cardiovascular system, and the body's general appearance. It also seems to bring calm, relaxation, and harmony to the mind. Performing the rites outdoors, in nature, creates a strong sense of connection with the environment that becomes even more intense when followed by a short meditation.

Learn about the five Tibetan rites and the related poses that make up the routine. I suggest performing the rites in the morning, preferably on an empty stomach. If the weather conditions are right, try to perform the rites in the middle of nature, in a place that you find suitable. Performing the Five Tibetans will give you an enormous amount of energy and a surprising sense of connection with nature and with your inner self.

THE FIVE TIBETANS

First rite: Stand up straight with your arms parallel to the floor, palms down. Keeping your eyes open and staying in one place, spin around slowly, in a clockwise direction. Keep your eyes on the ground without bending your head.

Second rite: Lying on your back, extend your arms on the ground along your sides. Inhale and lift your head, bringing your chin toward your chest. At the same time, lift your legs without bending your knees. Exhale and slowly lower your head and legs to their initial position. Relax all your muscles.

Third rite: Kneel on the floor with your knees shoulder width apart and your hips over your knees. Extend your upper body and place your palms on your lower thighs, under your gluteus. Inhale and lean back with your head, arching your spine to open your chest as you contract your gluteus. Exhale and lower your head forward, moving your chin toward your chest. Keep your hands on the back of your thighs or in your lumbar region as you perform the rite.

Fourth rite: Sit on the floor with your legs extended in front of you, with your feet shoulder width apart. Place your hands on the floor next to your side with your fingers pointing ahead. Straighten your trunk and lower your chin toward your chest. Inhale and delicately lower your head to the back. At the same time, lift your body and bend your knees until your trunk and thighs are parallel to the ground, letting your head bend slightly back. Contract all of your muscles, particularly your gluteus, and hold your breath. Exhaling, relax your muscles and return to your starting position.

Fifth rite: Lie on the floor on your belly and place your hands under your shoulders. Inhaling, curl your toes under and, pressing your hands and feet into the ground at the same time, extend your arms and legs and lift your pelvis into an upside down V shape, with your chin to your chest and your back as straight as possible. Then exhale and lower your thighs to the ground, keeping your upper body lifted, your chest open, and your eyes to the sky, in a cobra position.

With a Full Belly

Professor Martin Nyffler of the University of Basel in Switzerland conducted a study that showed that we share our planet with approximately 25 million tons of spiders belonging to 45,000 species. These spiders can eat more than 800 million tons of insects every year, collaborating with ants and birds to regulate the number of insects in the ecosystem. Every animal species contributes to equilibrating the populations of other species. Humans, on the contrary, feed themselves without regard for their ecosystems and sometimes destroy them.

Choosing what you eat is a way of establishing a relationship between ourselves and with the reality around us: nature, animals, people, and matter. We have to realize the importance of this relationship as soon as possible if we want to develop a strategy for long-term environmental sustainability.

At present, there are no prospects of significant change in food production and distribution systems that would lower environmental impact. This is primarily because of the huge number of people who must be fed every day, of the distraction or unawareness on the part of consumers, and of the industrialization of food production and distribution, all of which hinder the idea of significant environmental protections.

It may seem impossible, but there are some things we can do to limit the damage and impact on ecosystems, even if simply by carefully selecting the products we buy. Respecting the environment and pursuing actual environmental and social sustainability also means keeping endangered animal and fish species, out-of-season vegetables, and products that use underpaid labor and inadequate production processes off our table. We should also consider how our food is packaged when we choose what to put into our grocery cart.

At this point, our re-wilding journey includes asking ourselves questions when we venture into the realm of food distribution, and becoming aware of the impact that the production of what we buy has on the environment.

It really is not that difficult to find foods and products that consider the environmental emergency we are experiencing. Try to favor small local producers; it is also a way to support the social-economic fabric of our community.

Make a list of the things you could never do without in your diet, and try to understand the impact they have on the environment. Be informed about the seasonality of fruits and vegetables, and select only those that are produced nearby and distributed in-season. Try to avoid packaging that pollutes, and try to minimize the garbage you generate, whether it is organic or not.

165

Talking Rocks

The magma that boils under the Earth's crust is in constant movement. As it flows toward the center of the Earth, the temperature of the molten mass is much higher than that of the upper layers, causing a "convective" current, which pushes the deeper materials toward the Earth's crust, where they cool and descend back down toward the depths of the Earth. This continuous stirring is also the origin of the shift in the Earth's crust: when two plates pull apart, splits are created; and if the split reaches the magma, the molten underground rock tends to rise to the surface.

When the magma escapes and cools, the various components of its mass condense and separate, forming nuclei that then become large crystals. The material that makes up the magma determines the substances that will make up the minerals. Pressure, heat, space, and time determine the crystallization process.

During our walks, we can find stones with various kinds of crystals embedded in them. I suggest that you collect them and observe them carefully. It has been traditionally believed that crystals carry information and specific vibrations or frequencies that can condition or modify the vibrations and frequencies of other objects that they come into contact with, which is why crystals are sometimes thought to have healing properties, and that they can help guide the thoughts and lives of those who wear them.

The characteristics of the crystals, their color, their lithogenous formation and mineral class, determine their uniqueness and possible use. These characteristics are the result of transformations that can last millions of years. In this sense, each crystal is the pure expression of nature's generative mechanisms, a small treasure to be kept with great care.

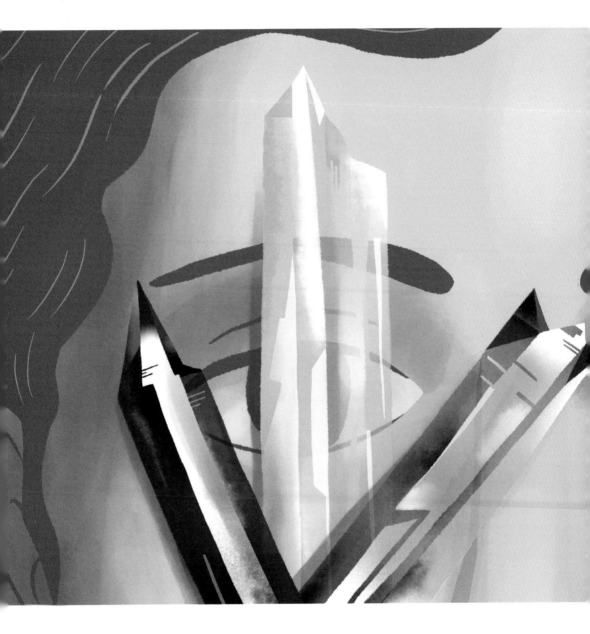

Learn about places near you where you might find crystals. There are many sources on the Internet on the subject. If you find a stone with an embedded crystal as you are walking, observe it closely and try to identify what kind it is. Take note of the location where you found it; you may have discovered a vein. Take only what you need, and leave the rest for those who come after you.

QUARTZ

Quartz is the most common mineral on the Earth; and although they have different names, many stones belong to the quartz family, including agate, jasper, chalcedony, and many others. The most important quartz deposits are found in Mexico, Russia, Brazil, Canada, the USA, Uruguay, Germany, and India. Hyaline quartz gets its name from the Greek word *hyalos*, meaning glass, but the ancient Greeks actually believed that it was frozen water that had become too compressed to melt.

In almost all cultures, quartz is considered a mineral with magic therapeutic powers, used in the past to repel demons and illnesses and to infuse strength and energy. In Medieval times, a quartz ball was thought to have hypnotic divinatory powers that could induce a trance in those who stared at it, allowing them to travel back in time and grasp the symbolic essence of the present and predict the future.

For some Native Americans and Burmese, quartzes were veritable living entities and, as an act of veneration, they offered them donations in exchange for favors during religious ceremonies.

Compiling a Library

Nature's wilderness has been described in many famous literary masterpieces, and each of us should compile a small library to hold the works of authors who are knowledgeable about the subject. Anyone who has experienced the emotions of living life in contact with nature has been inspired by the relationship. In addition to novels, there are extremely interesting essays that we can read and keep, as well as the biographies of great explorers. The words of those who have lived unforgettable adventures will always help us feel close to nature.

John Muir is the first author that will enrich our library; his works tell us of wonderful adventures set in the wilderness of the Sierra Nevada, in California. His direct activism helped preserve the Yosemite Valley and other areas, where his advocacy helped create several parks to protect the territory.

The second writer we must include is Henry David Thoreau, author of the famous book *Walden; or Life in the Woods*. It narrates his two years as a hermit immersed in the wilderness in a small cabin he built near Walden Pond, after escaping from the city and the materialism of society. This masterpiece allows us to experience an adventure made of slowness, of observing nature, of quiet walks, and of many reflections on the meaning of life.

Ralph Waldo Emerson is the author of *Nature*, a book in which he reflects on man's need to rediscover his role and reestablish a balance with nature through communion and unity with it.

Other great authors who have written about nature are Richard Mabey, with his masterpieces *Nature Cure* and *The Naturalist's Handbook*, Italo Calvino, with his wonderful *The Baron in the Trees*, Mary Oliver, with her poem *Crossing the Swamp*, and many others you will discover by browsing in libraries and bookstores or from talking to your hiking buddies, both present and future.

Dedicate one or more shelves in your library to books that
inspire you to experience nature in the best way possible—
through the imagination and example of great explorers.
Research the authors and volumes that you feel are
essential to nature literature.

Sharing Happiness

Leo Tolstoy wrote that happiness is real only when shared. With a similar vision, we can express the moral that closes the film *Into the Wild*, based on Jon Krakauer's novel of the same name. The book narrates the true story of Christopher McCandless, a photographer who leaves everything behind to live completely immersed in the wilderness, only to die from poisoning after ingesting a toxic berry.

Sharing the happiness of a hike in the company of others can be an exciting way to retrace a path we have already explored, or to take on a difficult challenge that we would not face alone. Sharing a path means sharing the effort, but it also means sharing the wonder of a notable place that becomes even more special when we visit it with others.

An important thing to consider as the organizer of an excursion is that you are responsible for all the members of the group, which means that you must take into account the capability of every group member when choosing your route. If they are not used to walking in nature, you must make sure they have suitable shoes, gear, and equipment for the predicted weather conditions. There are pleasant, scenic, easy trails that are within everyone's reach. Group members can help choose the trail and plan the excursion; it will help them feel involved and give them the chance to be excited about the trip before it even begins! We propose a clearly marked trail so that our friends can begin to learn to get their bearings on their own.

Find a group of people with whom you would enjoy sharing your hike or little adventure. Tell them the things you love about hiking, and try to convey the emotions you have felt previously on your solo outings. Tell them what you have learned about your re-wilding journey, and remind them that one of the best things about being in nature is the sense of community you get from it.

Like an Acorn

The oak tree is a symbol of power, of longevity, and of wisdom in many ancient cultures. It has been venerated as a divinatory plant with profound spiritual significance as well. Oaks grow all around us, and we should give some deep thought to these great plants and their acorns, and what they symbolize in our lives.

James Hillman, a world-famous Jungian psychoanalyst, philosopher, and writer, formulated the "acorn theory," a theory whose powerful psychological appeal to the dynamics of nature in the search for our path in life and in our role on the planet makes it very important to our re-wilding journey.

The theory states that the little acorn holds all the potential to become an immense, flourishing tree, and that the information it contains will determine the structure of the trunk, the bark, the color and shape of the leaves, the direction the roots will take, the branches and the acorns that the tree will produce, in turn. It holds that, in much the same way, when we come into the world, we already hold inside us our particular talents, our *daimon*, our role in life, and our natural destiny, and that it is up to us to identify and cultivate these if we hope to have a healthy, happy existence. But more often than not, this calling goes dormant and is forgotten, overwhelmed by rules imposed by society or wrong choices that lead us in other directions. So, although the acorn holds all the information and potential to become a great tree, it might rot before its time, or be eaten by an animal of the forest, or fall to other unexpected events. We must establish such a deep relationship with ourselves that it allows us to intuit our destiny, our true nature, and our role in the world.

⋮ **Reflect on the acorn theory.**

FROM THE ACORN TO THE OAK

In the Northern Hemisphere, where winters are harsh, January is a month when nature appears to be frozen and immobile; but in reality, seeds that previously fell to the ground are preparing to sprout and take root. The acorns that fell from oak trees at the end of summer slowly begin to sprout in the months of rain and mud that follow.

For woodland walkers like you, they are easily recognized. If you gather some acorns in the fall, you can wrap them in a wet paper towel, place them in a plastic bag, and leave them in the refrigerator for a few weeks, being careful that the paper towel never dries out. This process, called hibernating, convinces the acorn that winter has arrived and encourages it to germinate.

When you take them out of the refrigerator, the warmth will make them think spring has arrived, and they will rush to sprout. To watch it grow, hang the acorn over a glass or bottle so that the sprout is in the water and the acorn stays dry, or almost dry. You can use toothpicks to hang it over the water, or find a bottle with a narrow enough mouth. After a few months, the seedling will have created six or seven leaves, and in the spring you can plant it in the ground. Choose a suitable area, considering that the oak tree will become a massive plant over time.

Observing Micro-Seasons

During Japan's world-famous cherry blossom season, the streets and parks of the cities are filled with extraordinary colors. The Japanese have always been very sensitive to the ways nature changes over time, and in fact their customs, art, and literature have a poetic bond to animals, plants, natural habitats, and the weather. In Japanese culture, there are as many as seventy-two key moments of change and evolution throughout the year, each marked by a series of events that each highlight a particular moment in the natural cycle.

The Gregorian calendar considers only four fundamental positions of the sun, the equinoxes and solstices, which mark the four seasons, while ancient Japanese and Chinese calendars identify a much denser series of sun positions. These positions last for approximately fifteen days, making for a greater number of shorter seasons called *sekki*. The twenty-four sekki are also subdivided into other moments of about five days each that make up seventy-two short-lasting micro-seasons. Each of these sekki is characterized by delicate, almost imperceptible changes in nature, such as the arrival of the swallows, the days when mountain streams freeze, or the period in which rainbows are most frequent. Changes in plants and animals also characterize each micro-season, including the days when a particular flower blooms or a fish lays its eggs, or when a bird migrates or breeds.

Use your journal to make note of phenomena that have characterized nature around you in the last five to seven days. Describe the temperature, the precipitation, the clouds you have seen in the sky, the animals you have encountered on your walks, and their behavior. Moments such as the reawakening of animals from their hibernation, the appearance of blossoms on the branches, the freezing of mountain streams, or the sowing of wheat can all identify a micro-season. After a year, you will have your first draft of a Japanese-style calendar that describes a series of significant events in the nature that surrounds you.

THE MICRO-SEASONS OF SPRING

In the traditional Japanese calendar, spring is divided into the following seasonal micro-moments.

1) Risshun—The beginning of spring
February 4–8
Eastern winds melt the ice
February 9–13
Birds begin to sing in the bushes
in the mountains
February 14–15
Fish begin to peek out of the ice

2) Usui—The day the snow melts: rain
February 19–23
The rain moistens the earth
February 24–28
Banks of fog begin to appear
March 1–5
Buds sprout from the land and on the trees

**3) Keichitsu—The day worms come up
from the ground: insects wake up**
March 6–10
Hibernating insects come out
of their underground dens

March 11–15
The first peach blossoms bloom
March 16–20
Caterpillars turn into butterflies

4) Shunbun—Spring equinox
March 21–25
Sparrows build their nests
March 26–30
The first cherry blossoms bloom
March 31–April 4
Faraway thunder

5) Seimei—Serene and luminous
April 5–9
The swallows return
April 10–14
Wild geese fly north
April 15–19
The first rainbows appear

**6) Kokuu—The first rains begin to fall
and sowing begins**
April 20–24
The first reeds appear
April 25–29
The last freeze, rice plants begin to grow
April 30–May 4
Peonies bloom

Haiku

"A light rain falls, no noise, on the moss. How many memories of the past!"
Yosa Buson

In the seventeenth century, Japanese poets began using the *haiku* form of poetry to express the ephemeral, fleeting essence of nature—a ray of sunshine that suddenly lights up the leaves of a tree, the first drops of rain that fall on a meadow, or a branch bending in the wind. Although this form of poetry has evolved a great deal with respect to metric poetry, many people still use it today to express the similarities between human existence and the emotions that being surrounded by unspoiled nature triggers, and the small and often imperceptible signs of nature.

The name of this poetic genre was coined by the poet Masaoka Shiki, who also contributed to its great phase of development during the Edo period (1603–1868). Other great poets who contributed to consecrating the beauty of this poetic form, masterfully creating *haikus* to describe nature and human events related to it, are Matsuo Bashō, Kobayashi Issa, and Yosa Buson.

Commonly, *haikus* are written on a single line, with side-by-side images or concepts separated by a *kireji*, or "cutting word," which helps to define and separate the two poetic ideas or images. The poem needs no title, but it absolutely must have a direct or implied *kigo*, a reference to one of the four seasons. The connection can be extremely subtle or indirect, such as a reference to a weather event typical of a specific season or a specific region.

We can use this form of poetry to express our feelings when we find ourselves in front of the spectacles that nature offers us on our excursions. Being able to convey the emotions triggered by our contact with unspoiled nature in a few carefully chosen words means to deeply interiorize the state of mind that an intimate connection to nature gives each of us. Use your journal to collect your *haikus* and, if you want, add drawings that illustrate the feelings you are expressing.

When you find yourself in front of one of nature's wonders, something that excites you or triggers thoughts about human existence, the passing of the seasons, the wind, the rain, or animals, try your hand at writing a *haiku* to express the feelings that such images inspire in your soul.

Collaborating

One of the most important issues for nature lovers is understanding what active role to take in order to preserve our environment and its ecosystems. We can contact one of the many associations whose purpose is to protect the land, the seas and oceans, animals and biodiversity, and offer our time as a volunteer.

Donating a few hours of time for a cause we believe in can be very gratifying, as well as useful. In addition, our positive active behavior can also be an example for our friends and acquaintances, and can drive some of them who are undecided or a bit lazy to become part of the change.

Environmental associations play a fundamental role in our political system, dealing with issues for which the institutions often lack time and resources. These associations operate in various directions, doing many very different things, including awareness and information campaigns as well as concrete actions that promote greater respect for our habitat and the creatures in it.

The best idea is to find a small association near our home that is involved in a cause we care about; some protect both animals and plants, while others focus on specific environmental problems.

The large global associations are very important in creating political pressure on governments. They bring attention to the changes needed to achieve the goals of the global climate agendas or other priorities and transnational issues, but local associations are the ones that care about protecting the nature around us.

Organize your schedule and try to carve out a few hours to work with an environmental or animal-protection organization. Actively contributing to a cause will give you a chance to do something concrete for nature.

POACHING

Poaching is one of the biggest threats to plant and animal biodiversity, and consequently to all of us. The United Nations Office on Drugs and Crime (UNDC) estimates that seven thousand animal species are threatened by this cruel practice and by the illegal sales of the specimens that are captured.

Some commonly poached species are widely known, such as the panda, the African elephant, the tiger, and some species of whales; but the vast majority of them are little known, which makes it even more difficult to create strong opposition to the indiscriminate killing of so many animals.

There are certainly some endangered species in your area as well; during your walks, you may find a trap or some other mechanism put there to kill or capture a defenseless animal. If you find one of these traps or mechanisms, take pictures, notify the authorities, and make sure that someone deactivates it.

Rules for Sustainable Living

Living harmoniously with nature is both the cause and the effect of a healthy relationship with ourselves. To attain the state of mental tranquility and lasting satisfaction we all desire, we need to pursue a lifestyle that is sustainable for our planet and ourselves.

The first thing we must do is learn to maintain a calm, clear state of mind. We must learn not to be overwhelmed by confused, wandering thoughts, and we must become our own masters, uninfluenced by the opinions of others or by what is convenient or what society believes is "correct." Remember that the environmentalism that is now considered socially necessary was seen as snobbish or bizarre until just a few years ago. Developing a capacity for precise, orderly thinking is essential, so let's do one thing at a time and try not to get distracted.

Besides, expressing your will and taking initiative through carefully planned actions can improve our lives, the lives of those around us, and the health of our natural environment.

Commitment can also mean carrying out the practices illustrated in this book and reestablishing a strong connection with nature, fighting for animal rights, or clearing waste from natural lands. The actions we decide to take and their results, together with habitually checking that the feelings in our soul are well balanced, are the key to living our lives in peace. We must train our minds not to be overwhelmed by deep sadness or irrepressible joy.

In nature, balance is a structural concept that we can use to manage our existence, to maintain a positive attitude, to capture the beauty in what might even appear ugly, and to recognize opportunity even in the most negative occurrences. This requires withholding judgment and prejudice, and keeping ourselves open to the possibility that we may have to change our vision or opinion. Achieving this will be easier if we invest time in meditation and in cultivating gratitude.

Remember that there is no separation between ourselves and what surrounds us; we must consider nature as a part of, and an extension of, our being.

⋮ **Spend as much time as you can in wild nature.**

Bibliography

....

ARLETTAZ, R. – PATTHEY, P. – BALTIC, M. – LEU, T. – SCHAUB, M. – PALME, R. – JENNI-EIERMANN, S. *Spreading free-riding snow sports represent a novel serious threat for wildlife.* Royal Society Publishing, 6 March 2007

BARBIERO, G. – BERTO, R. *Introduzione alla biofilia. La relazione con la natura tra genetica e psicologia.* Carocci, 2016

CALVINO, I. *The Baron in the Trees.* Vintage Publishing, 2021

CHEVALIER, G. – SINATRA, S.T. – OSCHMAN, J.L. – SOKAL, K. – SOKAL, P. *Earthing: Health Implications of Reconnecting the Human Body to the Earth's Surface Electrons. Journal of Environmental and Public Health,* 2012

Declaration of the United Nations Conference on the Human Environment, Stockholm 1972, https://www.un.org/en/conferences/environment/stockholm1972

EMERSON, R. W. *Nature and Selected Essays.* Penguin Classics, 2003

GARDNER, H. *Frames of Mind: The Theory of Multiple Intelligences.* Basic Books, 2011

GNH Buthan, https://www.gnhcentrebhutan.org/history-of-gnh/

GOULD VAN PRAAG, C. – GARFINKEL, S. – SPARASCI, O. et al. *Mind-wandering and alterations to default mode network connectivity when listening to naturalistic versus artificial sounds. Scientific Reports,* VII, 2017

GOULD VAN PRAAG, C. *It's true: The sound of nature helps us relax. Science Daily,* 30 March 2017

HILLMAN, J. *The Soul's Code.* Ballantine Books, 2017

KEDLER, P. *The Eye of Revelation: The Ancient Tibetan Rites of Rejuvenation.* J.W. Watt, 2008

KRAKAUER, J. *Into the Wild.* Picador, 2018

LI, Q. – MORIMOTO, K. – NAKADAI, A. – INAGAKI, H.– KATSUMATA, M. – SHIMIZU, T. – HIRATA, Y. – HIRATA, K. – SUZUKI, H. – MIYAZAKI, Y. – KAGAWA, T. – KOYAMA, K. – OHIRA, T. – TAKAYAMA, N. – KRENSKY, A.M. – KAWADA, T. *Forest bathing enhances human natural killer activity and expression of anti-cancer proteins. International Journal of Immunopathology and Pharmacology,* Apr-June 2007

LOVELOCK, J. *Gaia: A New Look at Life on Earth.* Oxford University Press, 2000

MABEY, R. *The Unofficial Countryside.* Dovecote Press, 2010

MABEY, R. *Nature Cure.* Random House, 2018

NEIHARDT, J.G. *Black Elk Speaks. Being the Life Story of a Holy Man of the Ogalala Sioux, as Told to J.G. Neihardt, etc.* W. Morrow & Company, 1932

Nature of Americans, https://natureofamericans.org/

NYFFELER, M. – BIRKHOFER, K. *An estimated 400–800 million tons of prey are annually killed by the global spider community. The Science of Nature,* 2017

Overshoot Day, https://www.overshootday.org/

PASSMORE, H.A. – HOLDER, M. *Noticing nature: Individual and social benefits of a two-week intervention. The Journal of Positive Psychology,* 2016

SIMARD, S. – PERRY, D. – JONES, M., et al. *Net transfer of carbon between ectomycorrhizal tree species in the field. Nature,* CCCLXXXVIII, 1997

The Darwin Project, https://www.darwinproject.ac.uk/